Guide's Greatest
PRAYER
STORIES

Also by Helen Lee:
Guide's Greatest Miracle Stories

To order, call 1-800-765-6955.
Visit us at www.reviewandherald.com for information on other
Review and Herald products.

HELEN LEE, editor

Guide's Greatest

PRAYER

STORIES

REVIEW AND HERALD® PUBLISHING ASSOCIATION
HAGERSTOWN, MD 21740

Texts credited to NIV are from the *Holy Bible, New International Version.*
Copyright © 1973, 1978, 1984, International Bible Society. Used by per-
mission of Zondervan Bible Publishers.

This book was
Edited by Helen Lee
Designed by Madelyn Gatz/Trent Truman
Cover art by Corey Wolfe
Electronic makeup by Tina M. Ivany
Typeset: 13/16 Goudy

PRINTED IN U.S.A.

05   5 4 3

R&H Cataloging Service
Guide's greatest prayer stories,
        compiled and edited by Helen Lee

        1. Prayer—Stories.   I. Lee, Helen, 1976-

                242

ISBN 0-8280-1647-X

Contents

Introduction

Here are 24 of my favorite prayer stories from *Guide*, a weekly Christian magazine for young people ages 10-14. Read about Malcolm's ride on a mystery train, Kevin's narrow escape from a white-tipped shark, fast food for Rudy and his friend, and many other amazing answers to prayers.

Following the cover story, the rest are arranged in the order they appeared in *Guide*—from the 1950s and on through the decades. God has certainly been faithful!

I hope you enjoy these stories. And my prayer is that as you read this book, you'll learn to trust God with every detail of your life and to love Him as your best friend.

—Helen Lee

"Do not be anxious about anything,
but in everything, by prayer and petition,
with thanksgiving,
present your requests to God"
(Philippians 4:6, NIV).

1

Angelic Hanging

by Jenny Logan

My brother, Jeff, and I were playing cops and robbers in the blistering hot Bolivian sun. (We had moved to South America five years before when our father had become youth director and pastor of eight churches.) I was hiding under a large barrel, waiting for Jeff to come sneaking by.

Suddenly I heard the big iron gate creak. "Kids, come on inside the house. I have a surprise for you!" Dad hollered.

After the whole family had gathered around, Dad told us what the big surprise was. "We're going camping! I'm taking all of us up to the youth camp to stay for an entire month."

"A whole month?" Jeff and I shouted at once.

"Yes, and we leave tomorrow morning," Dad replied.

"Wow! I can't wait!" I exclaimed, jumping and leaping around the room.

"Jenny, calm down and start packing," Mom said.

"Good idea, Mom!" I raced out of the room.

Early the next morning, before sunrise, Dad woke us up. We hurried around the house, grabbing last-minute things we needed for the trip. Finally everything was loaded into our Jeep, and we were on our way.

The worst part of the three-hour trip was the road. It always scared Mom. In Bolivia the main highways are nothing more than one-car-wide dirt roads, and the road leading to Camp Lajos was especially dangerous. It was crooked and had a sharp upward grade. On one side of the road a cliff rose thousands of feet into the sky. On the other side a sheer rocky precipice plummeted down, down, down. At the very bottom a river rushed rapidly along the rocky floor of the canyon. But from the road far above, it seemed to be nothing more than a small creek trickling along.

The Jeep was barely narrow enough for the tires to stay on the road. Dad was silent, concentrating on driving. I could tell Mom was getting a little nervous. Finally she said, "Hey, kids, why don't we sing some camp songs? It'll make the time go faster."

She started to sing her favorite one, "On Top of Old Smoky." Soon everyone joined in.

I was standing at the back door of the Jeep looking out the window.

"Jenny, sit down!" Mom commanded. "I don't want that door to fly open and have you fall out."

Reluctantly I sat back down. "'Old McDonald had a farm . . .'" my brother burst forth exuberantly.

"'And on this farm he had a pig . . .'" I joined in.

We had sung just about every camp song we knew. The drive was getting long, and I had to go to the bathroom.

"Dad, how much longer?" I asked.

"Hush, Jenny, Dad's trying to concentrate on this terrible road. We'll be there soon," Mom said.

I was bored, and I didn't feel like singing anymore. Slowly I got up and walked to the back door of the Jeep. Peering out the window, I was soon absorbed in counting the little white crosses that dotted the side of the road. They marked the places where cars and their passengers had been hurled over the edge to their deaths.

My hands were splayed against the door when without warning the back door flew open. Thrown off balance, I grasped frantically for the handle and swung out with the door. The feeling of being suspended in thin air engulfed me. Panic set in.

"Mom, Dad!" I yelled. I twisted my head around to look at the Jeep. No one had noticed what had happened because of the usual rattle noises of the Jeep. I fearfully looked down. All I could see was the little creek thousands of feet below. I was hanging directly over the precipice. I gripped the handle harder, but I could tell by my sweaty palms that I was going to slip any minute.

"Dear Jesus," I prayed, "please help my mom and dad to see me, and help me to hang on tight."

I screamed again. This time my mom heard me. As she whirled her head around, her eyes widened in horror as she saw her child swaying like a rag doll over a jagged canyon.

"Lloyd, stop the car!" she said with all the calmness she could muster.

Dad glanced over his shoulder. A helpless expression spread over his face. He stopped the Jeep slowly so the door wouldn't slam shut with me in it. Then he ran around to the back door. He carefully leaned over the cliff, grasped the bottom of the door, and brought me to safety. I collapsed in his arms, sobbing with relief.

"I'm so sorry, Mom," I choked on my tears. "I'll never disobey you again, I promise."

Holding me tightly, she said, "I'm just glad you're safe, honey."

As I look back on that terrifying experience, there has never been a doubt in my mind as to how I was able to hang on to the handle. I know that my guardian angel was there right beside me, giving me the strength to hang on just a little longer.

2

Malcolm's Mystery Train

by Edgar A. Warren

Dad glanced at his watch for the tenth time in a half hour. "If we don't get to Charing Cross on time, we'll miss the last train to Watford," he said, shaking his head.

"What will we do then?" Malcom asked.

"I guess we'll have to spend the night at the Euston station. They have a very comfortable waiting room."

But Malcolm didn't want to spend the night in a train station. He wanted to sleep in his own bed, especially after a long day of fun at the beach.

That morning Malcom and his mom and dad had traveled all the way from Watford, England, to the Kent coast to spend the day by the sea. Now they were on their way back home. The train they were on would take them to Charing Cross. Then they would have to walk two miles to the Euston station to catch the train to Watford.

But something was wrong. Although they were traveling the longest straight stretch of track in the British Isles, the brakes on the train would go on every few minutes, and the train would stop. Even when the train did get going, it traveled very slowly—until it stopped again!

Malcolm was so tired that he couldn't keep his eyes open any longer. Soon he fell asleep with Dad's arm around him.

"Will we make it, Dad?" Malcolm asked as soon as he woke up.

Again Dad looked at his watch. "We might," he replied.

"I'm praying that we'll catch the last train from Euston," Malcom announced. "What time does it leave?"

"Midnight, son. According to the timetables there's nothing after that on a Sunday night."

Malcolm sighed, because just then the engineer applied the brakes again. At the rate they were going, it was obvious that they wouldn't make it on time.

Just as they feared, they arrived very late at Charing Cross—so late in fact that the last Euston train had already left. But as cheerfully as possible they walked along the deserted streets until they arrived at the Euston station and found the waiting room Dad had mentioned.

"Would you get me some water?" Mom asked Dad just before they settled down. "I'm really thirsty."

Dad got up, took the cup, and walked to the drinking fountain near the platform, where—a half hour earlier—they should have caught the last train to Watford.

A big London policeman stood in front of the fountain.

"Excuse me, sir. I'd like a cup of water," Dad said to him. Then feeling that an explanation was called for, he continued. "Not much fun when you arrive back from the seaside too late for the last Watford train."

"No, but have you?" replied the policeman. "What's that train standing there now?"

Dad looked, and to his surprise he saw that a train was standing at the platform. But was it a train to Watford? He looked closely. Sure enough it was!

Dad ran back to the waiting room and called out excitedly, "Come quickly! Follow me!"

Soon Malcolm and his mom and dad were hurrying themselves into the train. At 12:40 a.m. they pulled out of the station and arrived at Watford 40 minutes later.

The next day Malcolm's dad looked up the timetable, but the story was still the same. Last train from Euston to Watford on Sunday night—12:00 midnight.

Still Dad was not satisfied. The next time he was at the Euston station he stopped by the office. "When does the last train to Watford leave here on Sunday nights?" he asked the ticket agent.

"Twelve o'clock midnight."

"But surely there's another one?"

"No," said the official, "there's nothing at all after that!"

A special train in answer to a boy's prayer? Malcolm is quite sure of it.

Mystery of License Plate OL 710-050

by Nellia Burman Garber

James Long, student colporteur, stepped up beside his old blue Ford. His head ached, his feet ached, and nothing looked more inviting on that warm autumn day in 1930 than the front seat of his battered car.

As he walked around the car to unlock the door, James noticed that his rear license plate was loose. He stopped to straighten it, noting the license plate number OL 710-050.

Once he was inside his car the number kept flashing before him. OL 710-050. OL 710-050. *What's wrong with me?* James wondered. *Did I get too much sun today, or what?* He tried to stop thinking about it as he drove along, but the woods seemed to be plastered with license plates.

When he finally arrived in Garden City, Kansas, a

half hour later, the sun was beginning to set. James stopped the old Ford in front of his house and got out. "I need something to wake me up and to drive those crazy license plates from my head," he told himself. "Then I'll go back and start knocking on doors again."

After fixing himself a limeade, James settled back in an easy chair to enjoy the cool and refreshing drink. He laid his aching head back against the soft upholstery and closed his tired eyes. *I'll rest for just a moment*, he thought.

About an hour later James woke up with a start and glanced at his watch. "It's almost 7:00?" he gasped, leaping to his feet. "I have to get back to work. The evening is the best time to canvass, and by the time I get back to my territory it will be almost too late to make any calls."

He felt his pockets for his keys and muttered, "Where are my car keys? Did I put them down somewhere?" He looked all around but couldn't find them.

I must have left them in the car, he thought. He hurried out the door to look, but the street in front of the house was empty. James rubbed his eyes and looked again, but the car was not there.

He turned this way and that, not knowing which way to go or just where to begin to get his car back. Then once again the number OL 710-050 flashed before his eyes. Of course, he could call the police and report the theft and the license number.

But first James bowed his head and thanked the Lord for drilling the number into his mind all afternoon. He asked God to keep his car from any accidents and to help him find it soon. Then he hurried back into the house and phoned the police station.

When the officers arrived, they asked James a number of questions. Then they took him to the police headquarters, where busy radios had already alerted every police car in the area regarding the theft and the license number of the car.

James sat in the corner of the police station, his head in his hands. He prayed silently—for his car, for the expensive new books he had stored in it, and for God's guidance.

Then the radio reported that the car had been found and that two young men had been taken into custody. The officer ordered a wrecker to be sent to tow the stolen car in. James' relief that the car had been found was spoiled by anxiety over what had happened that made it necessary to tow his car, but he thanked God for a partial answer to his prayer and tried to be content.

Two hours later, when the old Ford had been towed to the police station, James sat and listened to the questioning of the two young thieves. They had seen the car with the keys in the ignition and had decided to take it. Everything was OK for about an hour, they said, and then all of a sudden the car just stopped and they couldn't get it to start. While they were working on the engine, a patrol car had pulled up behind them.

"Officer, may I ask them a question?" James asked.

"Sure. Go ahead," the police chief replied.

James looked at the two young men who had stolen his car and asked, "What time was it when the car started giving you trouble?"

"About 7:05," one of them answered. "I know, because Bud here asked me what time it was, and I looked at my watch."

"Any other questions?" the officer asked.

"No, sir," James replied, "but may I go out and see if my car will start?"

"Sure," said the policeman, tossing him the key, "but it's deader than a doornail. I made these fellows try it out several times because I didn't want to bother with a tow truck."

The county sheriff walked out to the car with James and watched as he slid under the wheel. As soon as James pushed on the starter, the motor immediately burst into life.

The sheriff whistled. "Now, how do you account for that? I *know* that car wouldn't run. I saw those kids try to start it. What's your formula?"

Then James told the policeman how at 7:05 he had prayed that God would get his car back for him and that at 7:05 the car had stalled.

"That's my formula, sir," said James solemnly. "God answered my prayer."

"Well, I never!" said the sheriff. He turned quickly and blew his nose. Yes, even policemen can be moved to tears when they see how God works for His children.

4

Gun Battle on Their Campout!

by Gladys King Taylor

Hey, Don!" David called as classes let out on Wednesday afternoon. "It's vacation till Monday. Let's go camping tonight before the weather changes."

"Sure, but we'll have to ask our mothers first," Don answered.

Don was 16, and David, a year younger, was already as tall as his father. But although they were old enough to take care of themselves, both mothers hesitated.

The boys lived in Cuba, and there had been a revolution there for many months. One of the worst battles had been fought right around the city where Don and David lived. The boys had a collection of machine-gun shells they had picked up in their own backyards.

Everybody in town had been impressed by the

longhaired, bearded rebel soldiers. They were friendly, tireless young men. And even now, though the fighting was over, groups of soldiers still patrolled the island. Some of the soldiers from the other side were also still at large. Camping under such conditions would be risky business.

But the boys were so eager that the mothers finally gave in and told them they could go. After all, they would be spending the night on a hill only five miles from home.

The two boys wasted no time getting out their sleeping bags and packing food for supper and breakfast. Then they began the five-mile hike with their backpacks. Ahead of them was the challenging climb up Pelo Malo.

"Look over there," Don said. "That farmer's staring at us."

"He probably thinks we're a couple of patrols," David laughed. "Wouldn't that be fun—to be taken for a couple of rebels!"

"But we don't have beards or long hair," Don said. "He knows we aren't guerrillas. But we could be mistaken for soldiers from the other side. And that could be bad."

"Walking across an open field in broad daylight? Wouldn't that be stupid!"

The boys soon approached steeper ground at the rocky base of Pelo Malo and started climbing. Talk subsided, then ceased almost entirely.

The ledge toward which the boys climbed formed part of a great cliff. Near the face of the cliff stood a huge upright rock. A smaller rock had fallen between the cliff and the upright rock. There was a tunnel under the small rock, about 15 feet long. Don and David knew that if they crawled through the tunnel, they would reach the ledge. And that's where they planned to spend the night.

"We made it!" David said as he stood up after crawling through the tunnel. "You know, a lot of people would think we're crazy to go through all this work just to sleep on a rocky bed. But they don't realize that a sunset from down there isn't half as magnificent as a sunset up here. It's like standing at the top of the world!"

"I think I'd feel better with a sandwich in my stomach," Don said, throwing off his pack.

"Let's spread out our sleeping bags first," David suggested. "Then as soon as we eat, we can lie down and watch the stars come out."

Shoes and shirts were off, beds laid out and ready to crawl into, and supper half eaten when suddenly a "whoo-oo-oo, whoo-oo-oo, whoo-oo-oo" sounded from within the cave. Both boys reached for their flashlights. Stealthily they approached the cave opening and shone their lights inside. Nothing.

"There must be an owl around somewhere," Don said. He settled down to finish his sandwich.

Then without warning there was a bang-bang-bang below the ledge. The whiz of bullets past their ears made both boys drop flat on their stomachs behind a boulder. Pieces of rock shattered above them. For a few minutes they were so scared they could hardly move. For what seemed an hour the shooting continued.

The boys prayed. They prayed individually, and they prayed together. They asked God to protect them from whatever danger they were in. Praying was the only thing they could do as they crouched close together behind the rock.

The sun had set about the time the owl hooted. Now the night was getting dark, and bullets were still bouncing off the rocks.

"It's really dark now," David whispered. "Keep on your stomach, and let's inch ourselves into the cave. We'll be more sheltered there."

Slowly, low on their stomachs, the boys pulled themselves to the cave and crawled in. There they sat and tried to figure out what had happened. They decided that soldiers from one side must be shooting, thinking that they were from the other side.

"If they stop shooting long enough to hear me yell," David said, "I'll tell them who we are. Maybe that will stop them."

"Dear God," they prayed again, "keep the shots

from hitting us while we yell, and please make the soldiers understand."

David kept his head low as he stuck it outside the cave and shouted. The shooting stopped. "We are not soldiers," he called in Spanish. "We are boys from the Adventist college, just camping out for the night."

What he said wasn't very persuasive. Camping out in the open country during a revolution was risky business. And people in Cuba didn't often go on overnight trips just for the fun of it. The boys would have to give a better answer for themselves.

"Come down one at a time," the commander shouted back.

"All right," David replied. He was afraid to turn on his flashlight, so he felt in the dark for his discarded shirt and shoes. He couldn't locate them, and he must not delay. He fumbled for handholds and footholds to descend the cliff, stumbling and rolling as he bounced down.

As he approached the men with the guns, the leader called, "Put up your hands, and come slowly."

David was shaking, but in his heart he was no longer afraid. He was sure God was answering their prayers.

The soldiers were not rough, but they searched him thoroughly. They asked his name, where he was from, how old he was, and many other questions.

Finally, when David felt they believed him, he

said, "There is one other boy up there. Neither of us has a weapon. We just like being in the open air and studying the stars at night. Is it OK to call him down?"

The captain nodded.

Since David had lived most of his 15 years in Spanish-speaking countries, he had spoken to the men in their own language. But when he called to Don to come down, he shouted in English. He heard the soldiers remark under their breath, *"Es niño americano* ["He is an American boy."]."

The soldiers were now convinced that David and Don were students. But there were still a few things they wanted explained.

While Don was coming down, David listened to the soldiers talking to each other. He learned that a farmer had sent word that two armed men from the other side had been seen walking toward Pelo Malo.

Soldiers were sent to go and fire at the cliffs to stop them. Meanwhile, more soldiers had been stationed on the far side of the hill. They too had fired at the cliffs, which made the guards on this side of the hill think that the "soldiers" up on Pelo Malo were firing back! They had sent to the city for reinforcements to come and help them take the hill by storm.

David looked at his watch for the first time since sunset. No wonder the shooting had seemed endless! More than three hours had passed from the "whoo-oo-oo" of the owl until now. He and Don, mistaken for two soldiers, had been shot at for nearly three and a half hours!

The captain seemed satisfied with Don's answers, so David asked if they could go back up and get their things.

"Not by yourselves," the captain said. "Two of my men will go with you."

None of the soldiers wanted to climb the steep cliff. Finally the captain picked out two men and sent them up with the boys.

One man had a machine gun and could not make it. He stumbled and rolled back. The other man had a rifle. He took it off and was able to reach the ledge in the light of the boys' flashlights. "You two fellows would make good mountain fighters," he said.

Shoes and shirts on, they returned to the rebel squad, and the boys were taken to headquarters. There the captain tried to get in touch with the Adventist school by phone. But it was late, and no one answered.

The friendly captain took David and Don in his own private patrol car the six-mile ride out to the school. It was nearly midnight when they arrived. The two boys were exhausted but thankful that God had answered their prayers.

5

God Turned the Lights On

by Velva B. Holt

t was the night of October 7, 1959. Without any warning the electricity had gone out, and the whole town of Grants Pass, Oregon, lay in darkness.

Mrs. Ray Kinch was babysitting in someone else's house, and she didn't know where to find candles. So here she was with four children and no lights. It was a rather frightening situation.

The 2-year-old baby was already in bed, and in a matter of minutes the rest of the children would have been tucked in and fast asleep. But now they couldn't find their pajamas and were too afraid to go to bed even if they could.

Mrs. Kinch hoped the lights would come back on soon. But in the meantime she put her arms around the crying children to console them.

"Don't be afraid," she said. "Jesus loves little children and takes care of them, even in the darkness."

At other times when she was babysitting, Mrs. Kinch had told Bible stories to the children. So even though their parents hadn't taught them anything about Jesus, they had heard about Him many times before.

Billy, the oldest child, was trying to be brave. "We can pray to Jesus, can't we?" he suggested.

"Yes," the others chorused. "He could make it light, couldn't He?"

"Yes, of course," Mrs. Kinch replied slowly. "He could make it light if He wanted to. But, you see, God doesn't always find it best to do everything just as we ask—"

"But we can ask, can't we?" the children interrupted. They wanted light, and they wanted it at that moment.

"All right," Mrs. Kinch agreed. "Let's kneel and ask God to make it light. But you must remember that we are praying for God's will to be done. And if it isn't His will that we have light just now, we shouldn't think that He didn't hear our prayer."

Holding the children close to her, Mrs. Kinch prayed, "Dear Jesus, if it is Thy will, make it light. But if not, then keep us safe through this awful darkness. Amen."

When the prayer was over, there was a knock on the door. This frightened the children even more.

Their parents had warned them not to open the door to any stranger, especially because there had been prowlers in the neighborhood recently.

Feeling somewhat uneasy herself, Mrs. Kinch called out, "Who is it?"

A woman's voice answered, "I'm a friend of the family and have brought you some candles."

The children immediately recognized who it was, and they thought this was the answer to their prayer. "Jesus did answer our prayer, didn't He?" Billy quickly commented.

Mrs. Kinch inched her way to the door. The friend who handed over the candles had not thought to bring matches, and she didn't know where to find any. After locking the door again, Mrs. Kinch groped along in the darkness until she finally found some matches to light the candles.

The 3-year-old girl was then put to bed. And although she usually cried for the hall light to be left on, she seemed to understand that she could have no light that night.

Mrs. Kinch stepped outside to see whether there were any lights around town, but could see none. Since there had been no storm to cause the power to go off, it was a mystery why the blackout had occurred and why it was lasting so long. Since their radio didn't work without electricity, there was no way of learning the reason for the power failure.

Over the kitchen table Mrs. Kinch told Bible stories to the older children. It was getting late, but she allowed them to stay up later than usual. She told them about the importance of light and that God had made the sun, moon, and stars.

"How did He make light, Grandma Kinch?" Billy asked.

"God made it in the very beginning," she answered. And she began to recite, "'In the beginning God created the heaven and the earth. And the earth was without form, and void; and darkness was upon the face of the deep—'"

"You mean it was all dark just the way it is now?" the children interrupted.

"Yes, it was very dark."

"But how did God make it light?" they eagerly questioned, wishing they had more than candlelight.

"Well, the Bible says, 'The Spirit of God moved upon the face of the waters. And God said, "Let there be light: and there was light."'" (See Genesis 1:1-30.)

At that very instant, lights came on all over the house!

The boys jumped up and down, shouting, "You said, 'Let there be light,' and all our lights came on! God *did* hear your prayer, and He gave us more light."

Mrs. Kinch wanted to make sure the lights were not on everywhere else too—that it wasn't just a coincidence that they had come on at that moment. So she stepped out onto the porch to take a peek at the rest of the town. The only lights visible were the scattered lights of cars and a few candles shining dimly from the windows of the nearest neighbors.

Mrs. Kinch went back into the house and turned on the radio. The local station was still off the air, and the electric clock, which had stopped at 8:00 p.m., had once more started but was 2 hours and 15 minutes slow by her watch. This meant that the lights had been off all that time.

Filled with a strange awe, Mrs. Kinch said, "Children, let's bow our heads and thank Jesus for hearing our prayer, and for taking care of us, for surely He has given us light."

When the power was finally restored all over town, Mrs. Kinch learned that an airplane had crashed into the main transformer, causing the worst power failure their town had ever experienced. And no other lights had come on that night until several hours later.

The children didn't forget to tell their parents about the wonderful things that had happened that night as God heard and answered their prayers. They told them of how Mrs. Kinch had repeated the Bible verse "And God said, 'Let there be light,' and there was light" (Genesis 1:3), and all the lights in their house had come on, but none in the rest of the town.

The parents were very impressed with what they

heard. And the light that shone through the darkness that night may have been God's way of letting His message shine into their darkened hearts so that they could see the light of His power in their own lives.

6

Tommie's First Prayer

by Thelma Norman

The bell rang, signaling the end of the school day. Seventh- and eighth-graders poured out into the hallway, talking excitedly among themselves.

Because there were no classes the following day, the eighth-graders had planned an excursion and had invited the seventh-graders to come along. Everyone was to be at the school at 7:30 the next morning, where a bus would be waiting. First they would visit a teachers' college in the next state and tour their museum and observatory. Then they would go through a bakery and canning factory. They would be back at the school at 10:00 that night.

"Tommie, do you think you can go?" Lucinda asked.

It was well-known that Tommie was seldom able to attend school functions. Her family lived back in the hills more than five miles from town, and their only transportation was a box wagon and a pair of mules.

Tommie looked doubtful. "If I had a way to get to the school and back, I'm sure my parents would let me go," she replied.

"You can ride in with us if your folks let you come over early in the morning," Lucinda said. "But I'm going to spend the next night in town with Laura, so you'd have to find another way home."

"Oh, thank you, Lu!" Tommie beamed. "Here comes my bus! See you tomorrow—I hope!"

Tommie's thoughts raced a mile a minute all the way home. Her Uncle Bill had a car, and she knew he'd be glad to come to the school the next night to get her. After all, she was his favorite niece, a fact he made no effort to hide.

But how would she get a message to Uncle Bill? He lived three miles from her home. *Maybe if I hurry and get my work done, and if I can find the cows without too much trouble, I'll have time to walk over and see Uncle Bill myself,* she thought.

Tommie's mother listened to the eager words as her daughter outlined her plans for the next day.

"And Mother, don't you think I'll have time to go over to Uncle Bill's and see whether he will pick me up tomorrow night? I'll hurry!"

"You'll have to ask your dad," Mother replied.

Tommie knew that her plans had hit a snag.

"No, you can't go over to Bill's tonight," Father said sternly. "Don't you remember what happened last night when you went after the cows?"

Tommie remembered all too well. While hunting for the cows the previous evening, she had found a tangled mass of string and had sat down on a log to untangle the snarls and wind the cord up neatly. So intent had she been on salvaging the tangled string that it was dark almost before she knew it. Then she had jumped up and hurried through the woods, listening for the cowbells, calling, searching. Finally she had given up and returned to the barnyard, only to find that the cows had returned home by themselves and the family had half the milking done. She had gotten quite a severe scolding.

"But, Dad, this is different," Tommie said.

"No, it isn't," he interrupted. "If you can't be trusted one day, how can I trust you the next? You can just consider this as part of your punishment. Now, go on and get the cows—and be quick about it!"

Tommie knew better than to argue with her father. She walked sadly to the pasture.

"Maybe Uncle Bill will come over to visit tonight and I can tell him," she mused out loud. "Maybe if I prayed, he might come. I've heard that God answers prayers. Lucinda and Dixie say it's true, and they both go to church. And that paper that Aunt Nola used to send me—I think it was called *Our Little*

Friend—had lots of stories about how God answers prayers, only they were all about little children. Maybe you're supposed to take care of yourself when you get as big as I am. Still, I think I'll try it."

She walked farther into the woods. "I think people kneel when they pray," she said to herself, "so that is what I'd better do."

She knelt down beside a small sassafras tree and said her first prayer. She explained that she didn't know much about praying, but she hoped God would understand. She told Him how badly she wanted to go on the trip the next day and how it all depended on Uncle Bill. She asked God if He couldn't fix it somehow for her to see Uncle Bill that evening—she'd be so grateful if He would.

Tommie knew enough about prayer to end with an Amen. Then she resumed her search for the cows. It wasn't long before she had them all in the barnyard.

After quickly finishing the rest of her work, Tommie began to get ready for the next day's trip. All the while she listened for the sound of a car. Her brothers came in after finishing the outside chores, supper was eaten, the dishes were washed, and still Uncle Bill hadn't come. Tommie grew more and more anxious.

Finally her father put down his newspaper and announced that it was time for bed. Shortly afterward he blew out the lamp, and the household settled down for the night.

Tommie was terribly disappointed. She knew that any hope of seeing her uncle that night was gone. People didn't go visiting after bedtime—not in the country where work starts in the morning before sunup.

Maybe there isn't much to this religion business, after all, she thought to herself. *It would have been nice to know that God answers prayers.* At last she fell asleep.

Suddenly Tommie was awakened by a loud pounding on the door and a voice that shouted, "Anybody home?"

That voice! It was Uncle Bill!

Tommie struggled into her clothes. She heard her father getting up and lighting the lamp. "Something must have happened," she heard her mother say, "or he wouldn't have come this time of night."

Tommie walked into the front room as her father opened the door. Uncle Bill was not alone; he had brought his whole family, even Granny, who lived with them.

"Is something wrong?" Tommie's mother asked anxiously. "It's late—why, it's after 11:00!"

"Oh, it's just some of Bill's foolishness," Granny said, half grumbling, half laughing. "The rest of us were in bed, and Bill made us get up to come over here. He said he couldn't fall asleep and was going to come over here to see if Tommie would pop him some popcorn!"

Tommie quickly told Uncle Bill about the trip

the next day and how she needed a ride home after it was over.

"Sure," her uncle said. "I'll come for you tomorrow night—if you'll pop me some popcorn!"

"I'll pop you a whole bushel of popcorn!" Tommie exclaimed.

"Better get started then," Uncle Bill teased. "That's going to take a while."

Tommie hurried into the kitchen and began building up the fire. Then she stopped. She should say Thank You.

"God, I'm so glad to know that You really do answer prayers, and You must care about me. Thank You so much! Someday I hope to find out more about You. Thank You again. Amen!"

Later, listening to the voices of the family in the front room and to the pop-snap of the popcorn in the pan, and feeling the warmth of the fire, Tommie mused contentedly over the happenings of the day. It was possible that what she had discovered that day could make a big change in her life. And she was right—it did!

7

Gift From Heaven

by Bertil L. Gilleroth

You pray night and day, but it doesn't do any good," Agge remarked as his mother rose from her knees. "The Lord doesn't notice us way up here in the mountains."

"Agge Holgerson!" his mother reproved. "God sees every little bird that falls. He will care for us, never fear. You must have faith."

Little Gustava sidled up and laid her head in her mother's lap. Agge wheeled around and strode out of the room. He could not bear to see the distress of his two younger brothers and his two small sisters. *He* could take it, he was older—but still, his stomach rebelled at the thought of another mouthful of dried fish.

Agge remembered the happy day when they had left their old house in the valley to make a home of their own in the mountains. With a few goats and all the necessities they could carry on their backs they had made their way on foot up the mountains where Father had obtained 800 *ar* (20 acres) of virgin land from the Swedish government.

The long trek had not been easy, but the labor of clearing land, erecting a house, and breaking the stubborn, rocky soil had been even harder. Agge well remembered the blisters on his hands after he and his father had finished the field for clover.

Mother and the younger boys had worked without complaint on the garden plot, thinking of the potatoes, carrots, and rutabagas it would produce. And in spite of the many tasks, Mother always took a few minutes each day to open the family Bible and read to her family.

This was a wild, free country, and the new home was *theirs*. They were blessed with fine crops. A beautiful lake supplied them with fish. And the woods yielded nuts and berries in abundance.

Then tragedy struck. Father was stricken with yellow fever and died a few days later. The family valiantly carried on, but Agge was bitter. Why did God let Father die? Surely He must have forsaken them.

Now here they were, struggling to survive the harshest winter Sweden had ever known. Blizzards and below-zero temperatures had come upon them before all the crops were harvested. Never had snow fallen so early in the season, nor the lake frozen over so soon.

In next to no time a foot of snow covered the garden, and before Mother and the children could find more than a few baskets of potatoes and carrots, a terrible blizzard drove them into the house. From then on, it snowed every day. Mother rationed the vegetables and used more goat milk and cheese.

When the skies finally cleared, the temperature dropped even lower. Agge and Leif desperately tried to dig through to the garden, but they were forced to give up. The soil was hard as a rock.

Agge put on his ski boots and walked into the kitchen. "Mother, I am going to the lake. I might be able to cut a small hole through the ice and catch a fish. Wouldn't a fresh trout taste fine? I'm so tired of eating dried fish."

Mother put her arms about her eldest son and drew his head close to hers. "The dried fish are gone," she whispered.

He stared at her in dismay. "What will we live on?"

"Shhh," Mother warned. "Don't let the others hear."

Agge beckoned to Leif, his 11-year-old brother. "Get your ski boots. We're going fishing."

Leif looked at Agge as though convinced that his brother had lost his mind. But at Agge's frown he obeyed, and the two boys, equipped with knives, hooks, and line, skied to the lake.

With considerable effort they managed to hack

through to the water, but the fish, unlike the boys, were not hungry. And the two boys went home discouraged.

They stopped at the goat shed and tore open a bundle of clover and wild-grass hay for Svartgeten, the black goat, and Vitgeten, the white goat. Both goats were thin and gave but little milk. The children missed the rich cheese Mother used to make when the goats had provided more milk.

"No fish, Mother," Agge reported as the two boys entered the house.

"I was afraid so," Mother said with a sigh. "You tried your best, and that is all anyone can do—except pray."

Agge sniffed rudely.

"I guess we'll have to eat potatoes without fish," Leif said, trying to sound cheerful.

But Mother's stricken look told Agge that the last potato had been used. He motioned to Mother and led her out to the goat shed.

"The time has come," Agge said. "We must kill either Svartgeten or Vitgeten. Leif and Gustava will cry for their pets, but it is better for them to cry than to starve."

"We shall not starve, my son. God will care for us," Mother said.

Agge did not argue. But he was thinking that if God did not intervene soon, He wouldn't need to. It would be too late. The pale, pinched faces of Gustava and little Greta worried him. Jan was so weak from hunger that he didn't care what happened around him. Leif was hardier. But Mother looked so thin and worn that Agge was sure she ate barely enough to sustain life in order to give her children a few more bites.

"Which one?" he asked, pointing to the goats.

"No, no, Agge," Mother said. "We must have their milk. The little ones need it. We have two measures of flour left. With that and the milk and some water I can make gruel that will keep us alive until God sends help."

Fourteen-year-old Agge straightened his shoulders and held his head high. "I am a man now," he said. "Give me some money, and I will go to the valley for supplies."

Mother's eyes brimmed full. "We have one *krona* [26 cents] in the house. The long trip to town would not be worth it. Wait, Agge. We must trust God and not complain so long as He makes the flour last."

"You are thinking about the story of Elijah and the woman who cooked the last of her meal for him," Agge said.

"Yes, son. God provided her with flour. In like manner He will provide for us."

"Mother, I don't understand how you can believe that when we are all starving. You pray and pray, and instead of getting food we are running out of everything. I tell you, praying doesn't do any good. Maybe God is angry with us for something."

"No, no, Agge," Mother soothed. "God is not angry with us, and He will not let us starve. Somehow He will keep us through this terrible winter. I am sure He will."

That night Mother prayed beside her bed. She did not get up from her knees until morning. At breakfast time Gustava and Greta licked their bowls for the last precious drops of gruel.

Mother stood by the window shielding her eyes against the sun's glare on the wet snow. She saw an unfamiliar object far out on the white field. What was that thing flapping in the wind? It seemed to be anchored to the ground, yet it waved back and forth incessantly. It was not a weed—all plant life had been covered long ago.

"Agge, come here," Mother said. "What is that?"

Agge stared. The strange thing waved like a beckoning hand.

Leif crowded between his mother and brother and gazed intently at the mysterious object. "It looks like a letter," he said. "A big brown letter. Doesn't it, Agge?"

Agge had to agree. But how could a letter possibly have gotten out there?

"Maybe it came from heaven," Leif suggested.

Mother closed her eyes, and her lips moved silently. Then she cried, "Go! Go!"

Agge and Leif rushed out the door and plunged into the newly fallen snow without thinking of boots. Leif sank to his waist, but the taller Agge struggled ahead.

"Go back, Leif," he commanded. "It's too deep for you."

Leif was too excited to obey. He lunged on weakly in his brother's broken trail.

Agge soon reached the object. It was a letter—a long brown envelope, anyway. It was sealed, but there was no address on it. The boys made their way to the house as fast as they could. They scarcely felt their cold feet.

Mother opened the envelope with trembling fingers. She gasped. Inside was 50 *kroner* [$13.40], enough money in those days to buy all the supplies two boys could carry.

Where the money came from is a mystery that has not been solved to this day. Possibly the wind carried it from a long distance. But Mother and Agge both know that God's hand guided it and caused it to fall where it did, right in their backyard, in sight of the window.

"I will never doubt again, Mother," Agge promised. "I believe it now. God *does* see us far up here in the mountains. He hears you when you pray."

8

Mother, What Are You Waiting For?

by Yvonne Davy

Mother, what are you waiting for?" asked the two girls.

Yes, what was she waiting for? Did she expect to see a shining angel with folded wings, such as one sees in pictures? Or did she think someone might suddenly appear—someone with a strong noble face and a kind smile? Mrs. Wood wasn't quite sure.

The Wood family lived in Kitwe, one of the largest copper-mining towns in Zambia (formerly Northern Rhodesia), Africa. Mr. Wood had lost his job when he had accepted the Sabbath truth, but the family had not faltered in their determination to follow Jesus. Before long Mr. Wood had decided to become a literature evangelist so that he could support his wife and three girls as well as lead people to Jesus and hasten the day when his beloved Master would return.

This Sunday afternoon the Wood family had spent the day visiting Granny Becker, a dear friend. The two older girls, Heather and Moira, loved Granny Becker's home. Since they lived in a city apartment, they appreciated a big yard where they could play. Interesting flowers peeped at them from unexpected nooks in the garden. A gnarled old tree simply begged to be climbed. And, of course, there were a hundred interesting things to see inside the house.

While the children were thoroughly enjoying themselves, their parents had an equally good time studying the Bible with Granny Becker. At last Mr. Wood decided they had better start for home, for home was more than 30 miles away, and little Sheila's eyes were already heavy with sleep.

They waved goodbye to Granny Becker, and the steady purring of the engine lulled the girls to dreamland. For once even Moira and Heather lapsed into silence.

It was 7:30 before they reached the tall, red block of apartments that was home to them. Father took the sleeping baby, and Mother gently woke the older girls.

Heather yawned. "I'm so tired I could crawl into a hole and fall sleep."

"Me too," Moira agreed wearily.

"Without even a bite of supper?" Father teased. "Mother will have a bowl of soup fixed in no time."

"That would taste great!" The girls brightened

up considerably at the thought of their mother's good food.

Up, up, up they climbed to the fourth story in the building, for there were no elevators. Sheila grew heavier with each upward step. At last the family stood outside their own door. Father felt in a trouser pocket with his left hand. Then he shifted his little girl and felt in another pocket.

"Did you lock the door?" he asked Mother.

"No, dear. You were the last one out," Mother replied.

"Yes, but I don't have the key, so you must have locked it. Look inside your handbag."

Mother opened her bag and searched carefully through everything. But the key was not there.

"Maybe I dropped it when I bought gas in Chingola—taking out change," Father said. "Here, you take Sheila, and let me take everything out of my pockets. The key may have slipped behind something."

Father handed the sleeping baby to Mother. Rather frantically he hunted once more, but the key was not there.

"Some people can open doors with a pocketknife," Father said, opening up his. Unfortunately he wasn't one of those lock openers!

"I know what I'll do. I'll run downstairs to Mr. Belligan. He may know what to do." Father turned and hurried back down the passage to the stairway.

"Mother, I'm tired," Heather mumbled. She was so weary that her face was taking on an ashen hue. Mother was worried. She certainly didn't want one of the girls to get sick.

Moira bent down, wiggled the knob, and twisted it. She pulled and pushed. But the door would not open.

"Why can't we ask Jesus to help us?" Moira asked.

"Well—" Mother hesitated. A locked door seemed so trivial.

"Mother, you taught us in our Sabbath school lesson the other day that if we want something, we must ask Jesus for it," Heather said. "Let's pray right now."

Mother and her two girls—for baby Sheila was still fast asleep—bowed their heads. Mother prayed, Heather prayed, and then Moira prayed. Moira added her own little bit to the end. "Dear Jesus, please open the door for us. We're so tired, and besides, we have to go to school tomorrow. And if we have to sleep out here in the hall, we won't be able to get up in the morning."

All was quiet as Moira's voice died away. Mother shifted Sheila to her other arm.

"Mother, what are you waiting for?" asked the girls.

"Well—" Mother really didn't know what she was waiting for.

"We've prayed. Don't you believe Jesus can help

us?" Heather said.

"Oh, no, not that, only . . ." Mother was afraid to say what she thought. If she tried the door and it didn't open, would that destroy the children's confidence in God?

"My Father, honor the faith of Heather and Moira," she prayed silently as she put her hand on the knob. One little turn—

And the door swung open.

"Jesus did it! Jesus did it! I knew He could! I knew He would!" Moira sang out exultantly as they stepped into their home and switched on the light.

"And He didn't need to send an angel or even another person this time. I guess it was like the way He opened the doors of the prison long ago," Heather said.

When Father and Mr. Belligan arrived with a bunch of keys, they found Mother busy preparing supper and the girls setting the table.

"But—but—how?" Father began.

"So you found the key in your handbag after all!" Mr. Belligan laughed.

"Find the key? No, Mother didn't find the key. We didn't need a key—"

"Jesus opened the door because we prayed." The girls interrupted each other in their excitement.

Mr. Belligan smiled indulgently, but it was obvious that he didn't believe.

"The girls are telling the truth," Mother remarked.

"We continued to try to open the door after you left us, Father, but our efforts were in vain. So Moira suggested we ask Jesus to help us, and—we're in!"

"I just don't understand that . . . don't understand that." Mr. Belligan muttered more to himself than to the family around him as he shook his head slowly. He retraced his steps slowly, meditating on the power of prayer.

And Moira and Heather said a very fervent blessing as they tackled their bowls of hot soup.

9

A Jeepload of Mechanics

by Mabel Hillock

C hug. Chug. Chug. Jerk. Stop.

The missionary looked glumly at the dials on the dashboard. Yes, there was gas. He tried the starter. No, the engine would not start. The car just wasn't planning to budge an inch.

"Not again," he groaned.

The old car had a habit of acting like this. It had supposedly been fixed several times, but now it had stopped once again.

Wearily the missionary stepped out into the hot Indian sunshine and lifted the hood of the car. He was a school principal and had never been much of a mechanic "back home," but here in the mission field he was learning fast!

Taking out the tools he had placed under the front seat for emergencies, he began to tinker with the stubborn engine. Spark plugs wrong? No, they seemed to be all right. The carburetor? It looked OK. What else could it be?

The missionary worked on, his once-white shirt getting greasier and his hands getting grimier by the minute. Soon the others who had been in the car crowded around, trying to help. But although they did everything they could to put a spark of life into the defunct motor, it looked as though the vehicle had given up for good this time.

The missionary sighed and climbed back into the car to get away from the blistering sun. He wished he had brought some water to drink, but he hadn't planned to be gone so long.

It had all started several months before when the missionary had returned home from a committee meeting. "They agreed to let us build a new duplex for our Indian teachers," he had told his wife.

And so after many long sessions with paper, pencil, and contractors, the work had finally begun. Men had to dig out the foundations for the walls. And while they were doing that, stones were hauled to the site on bullock carts. Sand had to be dug from the riverbed behind the boys' dormitory and sifted. And permits had to be secured for everything—permits for stones, permits for sand, and permits for cement.

The missionary made seemingly endless trips for this, that, and the other. Now it was bricks that were needed, but there were no bricks to be found near the school. It was Divali season (comparable to Christmas and New Year in other countries), and no one would be making bricks until after Divali—which lasted nearly a month.

Finally someone told the missionary of a brick-yard several miles away where he could buy the bricks he so badly needed. So on a hot Friday after-noon the missionary, along with the school trea-surer, the contractor, and one or two of their friends, had piled into the car and started out to see what bricks could be bought.

But now they were having car trouble! They hadn't even reached the brickyard yet, and the pre-cious Friday afternoon hours were slipping away. Soon it would be Sabbath, and the men should be back at the school.

The missionary closed his eyes and silently prayed. "Dear Lord, please help us. You know I want to be home before sundown and I can't get this car to go. There isn't much traffic on this lonely road and no one I can turn to for help except You. Please make this car run."

He tried the starter again.

Buzz.

Silence.

He tried again.

Another buzz.

More silence.

The missionary leaned against the door and tried to figure out what he should do. He could walk several miles to find a mechanic, or perhaps one of the few passing trucks would tow—

Suddenly there was the roar of a motor, then the screeching of brakes as a jeep pulled up beside them. The missionary looked up to see men jumping out of the vehicle and walking toward him. How so many men could come out of one jeep amazed him.

"Are you having difficulty with your car?" one of them asked. "May we help you? We are all mechanics on our way to a convention."

With a whole jeepload of mechanics, it didn't take long to find and fix the problem. Soon both car and jeep were on their way again.

"The Lord does hear and answer our prayers," the missionary concluded when he told the story at vespers that night. "Sometimes in very unexpected ways!"

10

"I'll Pilot if You'll Pray"

by Harold Baasch

Ceiling 9,000 feet. Visibility six miles. Surface winds 30 knots . . . Altimeter three zero zero four. Taxi north. Cleared for takeoff."

The plane shuddered as the pilot, Jim Jackson, applied power. Looking out the window, David Fowler watched the ground roll back faster and faster and slowly drop away as they became airborne. The setting sun reflected on the lower side of the wing as they banked, heading for the huge range of mountains to the east.

"Are you sure we can land on the highway at Mante in the dark?" Elder Fowler asked.

"Sure," the pilot replied confidently. "We'll have a ceiling of 9,000 feet, which means the sky will be clear at that altitude. With no clouds and a six-mile visibility, there should be no problem at all."

Elder Fowler sat back in his seat to enjoy the rest of the trip. As the union president, he had scheduled to visit a mission in the northeastern part of Mexico. During their flight from Mexico City, they had encountered several delays, which forced them to fly at night in order to reach their destination, Mante. Elder Fowler had wanted to wait until morning, but Mr. Jackson had assured him that with such a high ceiling and good visibility, flying would be no problem.

Climbing to 12,000 feet to get over the mountains, the plane was soon enveloped in clouds. Mr. Jackson frequently glanced at the instrument panel, making adjustments when necessary. Every few minutes he flipped on the radio and got his position from the San Luis Potosi control center.

Elder Fowler sat next to him, his face reflecting the soft red glow of the panel. Except for the blurry image of a red or green light on the tip of each wing, nothing could be seen outside. The steady, monotonous drone of the engine was the only reminder that they were flying.

"We're almost there." Mr. Jackson's statement woke Elder Fowler. "I think we're directly over Mante, so we'll start spiraling down."

Slowly the plane banked and started circling, losing altitude with every round. Inside, the little hand on the altimeter recorded the steadily diminishing distance between the plane and the ground.

"Ten thousand feet," Mr. Jackson said. "According to the weather report we should break out of this cloud at about 9,000 feet and be in clear atmosphere."

Reaching behind the seat, Elder Fowler got his briefcase and then flipped on the interior lights. He leafed through the papers until he found the one with the names and addresses of the Adventist workers at Mante. Then he settled back in his seat and looked out the window. All he could see was a fuzzy light way out on the tip of the wing.

"Jim, we'll stay in Mante until the middle of tomorrow afternoon and then go on to Montemorelos, OK?"

"That's fine. You're the boss."

The only hint of movement was the moving hand of the altimeter as the plane lost altitude. Elder Fowler yawned frequently to pop the pressure in his ears.

"Nine thousand feet. We should break out of this any minute now," Mr. Jackson announced.

Looking out his window Elder Fowler hoped to see the lights of the small town below. But again, all he saw was the blurred wing light—blurred because the plane was still in clouds. Looking back at Mr. Jackson, he noticed that he was staring intently at the altimeter.

"What's wrong, Jim?"

"Looks like the ceiling's dropped. We're at 8,000 feet and still in clouds."

Both men turned and looked out. Neither spoke for a long time.

"Six thousand feet," Mr. Jackson said slowly.

"Clouds are thick as ever," Elder Fowler commented. "Jim, are you sure we're over Mante?"

"I'm pretty sure. I got my position when we started descending, but I'll check again." He flipped on the radio and picked up the microphone. "San Luis Potosi, this is zero six lima." (The call letters of the plane were 06L.)

"Come in, zero six lima."

"Request weather report for Mante area and position of zero six lima."

"Position of zero six lima, one mile southeast of Mante," the voice on the radio reported. "Weather for Mante and area, ceiling 9,000 feet."

The two men sat staring out at the darkness.

"Four thousand feet," Mr. Jackson muttered. He peered out the window for the first clue that they were out of the clouds. But the lights on the wing tips were still as blurred as before.

"I don't know what's happened, but we can't turn back," Mr. Jackson said. His voice had lost its reassuring confidence. "I'll pilot this plane if you'll pray."

Elder Fowler realized that they were in serious trouble. They *had* to land, but were they over Mante? If not, what was the ground like? How far down did this cloud layer go? Realizing that he could do nothing to help the pilot, Elder Fowler began to pray to the God who had saved him before.

"Two thousand feet. I don't know how far down to go and be safe," Mr. Jackson said grimly.

Each man, praying his own prayer, sat silent in the circling plane. Mr. Jackson continued to slowly lose altitude. "One thousand feet."

Neither man spoke. Both focused their attention on the altimeter as the hand moved, showing their continuous, steady loss of altitude. Nine hundred feet and still in the clouds. Mr. Jackson looked out at the fuzzy light on the wing. Suddenly it cleared. Taking his gaze from the light on the wing to what was below, he saw a small cluster of lights just to the north. That was Mante. The altimeter read 800 feet.

Taking a deep breath, Mr. Jackson shifted in his seat. "All we need now is some light on the highway, and we can land," he said.

The little plane circled the town a few times until a man down below, who had flown before, realized that the plane needed light on the highway. He gathered as many cars and trucks as he could in the little town and lined them up along the side of the highway with the lights on.

Mr. Jackson made a wide circle and lined up for landing. Suddenly Elder Fowler felt the plane go into a steep climb.

"What happened, Jim?"

"A truck pulled out onto the highway where I wanted to land. I'll have to make another approach."

Corning around the second time, Mr. Jackson lined up and started losing altitude again. Seeing that the road was clear, he set the plane gently on the highway and taxied to a halt, thankful that God had answered their prayers.

Early the next morning the two men left their little motel room to put their luggage in the plane before visiting the workers there at Mante. Mr. Jackson walked to the road to see where they had landed the night before.

"Dave, come here." His voice was tense. "Look!"

Elder Fowler walked over. When he saw what Mr. Jackson was pointing at, he stopped. There crossing the highway where they had landed the night before were a huge series of high-tension wires.

"We pulled up and landed under those wires," Mr. Jackson said. "I don't know how we missed hitting them."

The two men turned and went back to their hotel room. There they again thanked God for protecting them the night before.

11

The Doctor Prayed

by Peggy Dawkins

O Father, if it is Your will, please heal this poor woman."

As the doctor finished his earnest prayer he opened his eyes and for one brief moment looked through the window of the operating room. There was a look in his dark blue eyes that seemed almost like despair. How he wished he could do something to save this woman who was lying unconscious on the operating table.

If only she had not gone to the witch doctor! If only she had come to him sooner! But now it was too late. There was nothing, medically speaking, that he could do to save her life.

Asaria Nyakura was her name, and she was a very sick woman. For several months she had had a swelling in her abdomen. At first she had done nothing about it. Then when the swelling had grown very large and the pain was almost more than she could bear, she had walked many miles over the hills to the witch doctor, as was the custom of her people.

The witch doctor had thrown his bones and made a lot of strange concoctions with roots and blood and sand. He had uttered many weird sounds and incantations. But the pain had not gone, and the swelling had grown larger.

Asaria cried out in agony. She couldn't sleep, and she couldn't eat. Every day she grew weaker, and she knew she was going to die. Many of her friends told her to go to the mission hospital, but she was afraid to trust herself to the care of the missionary doctor. To do that would make the spirits angry, and she would have no peace again in this life. Yet she longed for help. If only someone would bring relief on her pain-racked body!

At last, after many days, she allowed her friends to take her to the mission hospital on the hill. How beautiful the hospital looked! It was all white, and in the clear African sunlight it looked clean and friendly. The lawns and the gardens were neat, and there were lovely flowers growing here and there. She felt at peace as she was carried through the front door and laid tenderly on a bed.

But now she was lying on the operating table in a deep anesthetic sleep, and the missionary doctor was sewing up the incision he had made. His examination showed that she had a large tumor in her abdomen, and the doctor knew it had gone too far for him to do anything to help her. He did not dare cut the tumor out. That would kill her for sure. But to leave it in—that would kill her too. He had left it in.

Again the missionary doctor prayed: "I have done all I can, dear Father. If it is Your will, You can still heal her and restore her to her family."

Back in the ward, Asaria was given loving care and tender treatment. No one expected her to live, and the nurses could do nothing for her but make her as comfortable as possible. Every day they prayed with her and told her about the Saviour who loved her and wanted to save her. Every night they showed her pictures of that same Saviour and asked Him to care for her while she slept.

After a few weeks of good nursing care and nourishing food, Asaria was still alive. Not only that, she was able to leave the hospital although her abdomen was still terribly swollen. The doctor sadly watched as Asaria made her way down the dusty road and disappear into the bush, where she would probably die.

Several months went by, and activities at the hospital continued at a busy pace. Every day new patients were examined and admitted to the wards, and every day they received tender care and love from the dedicated missionary doctor and his nurses.

One evening, pictures were to be shown in the large hospital dining room. An announcement went out to the villages nearby inviting the people to come. In they came, for they loved to see pictures on the screen.

The doctor sat at the back of the large room and watched as the people passed by and took their seats. He had helped many of them, and they showed their respect and affection for him as they greeted him. The men smiled broadly and clapped their hands. The women curtsied shyly, not daring so much as to raise their eyes from the ground.

One woman's face made the doctor think. He knew he had seen her before. But who was she? Where had he seen her? The pictures had already started when he suddenly remembered. Yes, she was the woman with the large tumor! She was the poor African woman he could do nothing to help—the one he had watched disappear into the bush to die. But here she was, after all these many months, looking well and strong.

The doctor was puzzled. He could hardly wait until the pictures were finished. He wanted to speak to the woman.

When the pictures were finally over, the doctor hurried across the room.

"Yes, I'm the woman who had the tumor," she replied. "But it's gone."

"Gone?" said the astonished doctor, hardly daring to believe his ears.

"Yes, the swelling and the pain are gone."

The doctor took her to his office and examined her carefully. There was no trace of the tumor. God had heard and answered the prayers of a dedicated missionary doctor.

12

At the Bottom of a Well

by Enola Chamberlin

My brother and I had no business being anywhere near the well a farmer was digging in a field. But my brother was upset with his friends, and he told me he was going to run away for good. I didn't like the thought of never seeing my older brother again, so I followed him.

The two of us, ages 9 and 6, trudged along until we were beyond the farthermost house of our little town, and then we walked on out over a country road. After we'd gone about two miles, I started crying and begging my brother to go home.

But my brother crawled under a fence into a field and started to run. I stumbled after him as fast as my short legs and my continual crying would let me. But soon I gave up, sat down, and cried. After what seemed like a very long time, my brother came back.

"If you'll stop crying, I'll show you something," he said.

Wiping the tears from my face, I jumped to my feet and followed him. And there, out of sight of any house, we came to a well. Boards had been laid loosely across the top of the hole. A windlass stood above it, with a rope leading down and out of sight between two boards.

My brother removed the boards from one side, and we looked down into the dirt pit perhaps 12 feet deep.

"I'll pull up the bucket," my brother said, "and give you a ride in it."

He unfastened the crank from a leather holder and began to turn the windlass. He had to stand on some wood in order to hold the crank when it was at the top of the turn. When he got the wide-mouthed bucket to the top, I crawled inside.

My brother let the handle slip until I was halfway down. Then he started to pull me up, but his weight and strength were not equal to the job. After a while he couldn't even hold me. I went down in little jerks until the bucket hit the bottom.

It was dark down in the pit, and I was frightened. I screamed to be pulled up. When nothing happened, I screamed louder.

What my brother should have done was go for help, even though he would have had to go a long way since there were no houses in sight. But he didn't want anyone to find out, for fear of being punished. And he was afraid my screaming would bring some-one. He had to stop me somehow.

My brother fastened the windlass crank and took hold of the rope. He thought he would let himself down easily, but his arms were tired. He came down fast, burning the palms of his hands.

"If you stop screaming, I'll get you out," he told me.

I quieted down, and my brother started to climb back up the rope. He might have made it if his hands had not been so sore, but he tried and tried until he was exhausted.

It was pitch dark now, and the sky we could see above us was a night sky. I didn't realize how serious our situation was, but my brother did. He could tell that no one had been working on the well for weeks, perhaps months, and that it might be months more before anyone came around. He also knew that although our folks and everyone in town would be hunting for us, they would have no idea where we were.

"Holler as hard as you can," he told me.

We shouted and shouted, the sound filling the space around us. But after a few minutes we realized that no one could hear us.

My brother started yelling at me that it was all my fault because I'd followed him. "We're going to die right here. No one can save us," he shouted.

The words *die* and *save* made me remember something that had happened a few months before. Our 2-year-old baby sister had become very sick, and the doctor had given up all hope. Our folks sent us, sobbing uncontrollably, to a neighbor, who quieted us, washed our tear-streaked faces, and set us on our knees beside a couch.

"We must ask God to save your sister," she said, kneeling down beside us. "Just say, 'Please, God, save our sister.'"

She prayed silently, but my brother and I prayed out loud, saying over and over, "Please, God, save our sister."

I believe that our prayers reached God and He honored them, because it was at the time we were praying that our sister started getting better and lived.

As we stood in that dark pit, I said to my brother, "Maybe we should ask God."

This made him remember too, so both of us began to ask God to save us. For a long time we said the words quietly as we had done before. Nothing happened.

"Maybe He can't hear us from down here," I said. "Maybe we should talk louder."

So we did. At first we talked in normal tones. Then presently we were shouting. We yelled so loud the words seemed to be bumping around in the narrow enclosure.

"Please, God, save us! Please, God, save us!" we screamed.

I was getting hoarse and exhausted and beginning to cry along with my shouting when my brother put a hand over my mouth. Then I heard what he had heard, the barking of a dog. So what? A dog couldn't get us out of the well. But my brother knew that where there was a dog, there would probably be a person.

"We're down here, down in the well," he called.

The dog was now right above us, barking furiously. Still no one came. Then we heard a man's voice telling the dog to come back.

"Yell," my brother said. We both yelled. Then the man's voice was right above us along with the dog's barks.

"What's down there?" he asked.

"We're down here," my brother answered.

"Please save us, God. Please save us," I kept shouting.

"Stay right there; I'll be back," the man said.

"It's all right now. It's all right," my brother said, trying to stop my wailing.

Then there was a lantern. Then came a ladder. Finally the man climbed down and carried us out.

Though the whole town was searching for us, the man was on his way into town from a more distant farm and had not heard of our disappearance.

"The well was abandoned," I heard him say. "No one might have come near it for months. If it hadn't been for my dog—" And that was the last I knew until morning.

Some people may say that it was just our shouting that brought the dog. But to me this experience was one more bit of evidence that God hears and answers our prayers.

13

Mrs. Mason's Miracle

by John D. Dorland

Pastor Webster stood at the church door, shaking hands with everyone after the Sabbath morning church service.

"Glad to see you here today, Brother Wilson."

"Sister Jordan, how is your husband? Tell him I'll be along to see him tomorrow afternoon. Room 31, isn't it?"

"Why, Brother and Sister Richmond! So nice to have you back. How did you enjoy your vacation?"

As a little gray-haired woman shyly approached, Pastor Webster thought hard to remember her name. "I hope you received a blessing this morning, Mrs. Mason," he said as he took her small frail hand in his large firm one.

Her voice trembled slightly. "Pastor, would you please show me your Bible?"

"Of course, Mrs. Mason. If you'll just wait until I've finished greeting everyone, I'll be happy to show it to you."

When the last member had passed him, Pastor Webster took his Bible from the shelf where he had left it and walked over to Mrs. Mason, who was waiting patiently at one side of the foyer. "Here it is, Sister Mason."

Mrs. Mason carefully took the big Book and stroked the soft black leather of its cover with her hands—hands that had been much more familiar with mops, brooms, wash buckets, and scrubbing brushes than with books. She had cleaned offices most of her working life.

Reverently Mrs. Mason opened the Bible and turned its pages, pausing once or twice to run a wrinkled forefinger along the line of the large clear type. Then she closed the Book, longingly caressed the gilt edges of the pages, and placed it back in Pastor Webster's hand.

"Pastor, could you please get a Bible for me, just like yours—exactly like yours?" she whispered.

Pastor Webster was a little taken aback. He liked his Bible and had bought a good one. Only the best, he believed, was good enough for the Lord's service. Twenty-five dollars was a lot to pay for a Bible, and he wondered if this little widow, existing on a small pension, would be able to afford it.

He paused a moment before he answered, "Certainly, Mrs. Mason. I can get one for you, but it's expensive."

"Oh, Pastor, don't worry about that. Just get me a Bible exactly like yours. And thank you." Her crinkled face broke into smiles as she spoke.

"I'll do it first thing on Monday," Pastor Webster assured her. "You'll have your Bible after prayer meeting Wednesday night."

So Wednesday night, right after prayer meeting, Mrs. Mason again waited until the others had gone. Then Pastor Webster gave her a large box with a golden cover. She opened it slowly as if savoring each precious second of the experience. Inside, faintly visible through its white-tissue wrapping, lay the Bible.

Carefully Mrs. Mason removed the Bible from the box, undid the tissue paper, and gazed at her new Bible as though she couldn't believe it. It was exactly the same as the pastor's. Then she set it down, opened her purse, and extended a roll of worn and crumpled dollar bills to Pastor Webster. "I hope this is enough, pastor," she said.

Surprised by its thickness, Pastor Webster took the roll and counted it. There was nearly $50. "Why, sister, this is almost twice as much as the Bible cost." With a smile he counted out $25 and returned the rest to Mrs. Mason.

"Pastor, thank you so much for buying me this

Bible." Eyes shining, Mrs. Mason clutched it to her heart with both hands. "Now, pastor, I want you to pray for me. I want you to pray that the Lord will teach me how to read. Will you do that?"

"Of course I will, Mrs. Mason," Pastor Webster replied, wondering for just a moment if this wasn't asking rather a lot of the Lord. Mrs. Mason was more than 70 years old and had never had a day of schooling in her life. It would be a miracle indeed if this woman learned to read. But Pastor Webster had promised to pray, and pray he did.

Week by week Pastor Webster saw Mrs. Mason arrive at church, her precious Bible in her arms. And week by week she gave him the same shy smile as she shook his hand after the service. But she rarely said a word.

Then one Sabbath, about a year after the purchase of the Bible, Mrs. Mason paused again as she left the church after the service. "Pastor, may I speak to you for a moment?"

Again she waited until the pastor had finished shaking hands. When he approached her, she was absolutely beaming. "Pastor, thank you so much for your prayers. The Lord has answered them."

"Prayers, Mrs. Mason?" Then suddenly recollection dawned. "You mean you can—"

"Yes, pastor, I can read. I can read my Bible!"

And then she told him how it had happened.

Each week during the sermon she had sat next to a friend. When Pastor Webster read a text, Mrs. Mason asked her friend to guide her finger so that it pointed to each word as the text was read. Gradually the words became familiar, and somehow she began to understand them just by looking.

"I don't know exactly how it happened, pastor. You know I've never had a single day of school in all my life. But God has answered my prayers and yours, and today I can read my Bible. Listen, I'll show you."

As Pastor Webster stood there listening to Mrs. Mason reading her Bible, watching the joy in her face, and hearing the delight in her voice, he blushed at his own lack of faith in the power of God.

Mrs. Mason finished reading and closed her Bible, but she had not finished smiling or talking. "And pastor," she went on, "I've been reading my Bible to some of my friends. There's Mrs. Ferger across the street, and Mr. and Mrs. Waring next door. I'd like you to visit them because they want Bible studies."

Bible studies they wanted, and Bible studies they received. No one in the whole church was happier than Mrs. Mason on baptism day.

Soon it became quite a common event for Pastor Webster to give Bible studies to a friend of Mrs. Mason's. And as time went on, he found that he didn't have to spend as much time explaining what the Bible taught.

"Oh, Mrs. Mason showed us that," they would say. And they would quote chapter and verse to prove it.

Mrs. Mason was really giving full course Bible studies in her own right. And when Mrs. Mason passed away, there were many in her church who owed their membership to the little gray-haired woman who had faith that the Lord could teach her to read.

14

Water Out of the Rock

by Deborah Cavel Greant

The sun rose slowly over the desert horizon, bringing with it the promise of another extremely hot day. Uncle John walked into the large old farmhouse kitchen, a look of worry on his face.

He waited for a moment before he spoke to Aunt Etta. "The well's dry," he said. "There's no water left in it at all."

Although it was only 4:30 in the morning, the temperature was already almost 100 degrees. Perspiration trickled down his neck and soaked into his collar.

Uncle John and Aunt Etta were used to being up before the early summer sun. It took a long time to prepare breakfast for 35 hungry children. And the boys and girls had to eat in two shifts because there weren't enough chairs, tables, or dishes.

Several years had passed since Uncle John and Aunt Etta had bought the old ranch with the dream of opening a children's home for otherwise homeless youngsters. Now the old place practically jumped with the happy shouts of the children who had come to live there.

Uncle John walked over to the telephone. "I'll borrow the water truck from town and haul water, but that will leave you to handle the work alone. Can you manage?"

Aunt Etta nodded. "The older ones will help. But what about the well? We can't afford to have a new one drilled."

"I'll talk to the driller this afternoon. Maybe he can come and look at it anyway."

Uncle John completed his call and headed out the door. Aunt Etta went about her work with a heavy load on her heart. God had held them in His hand for so many years. Surely He wouldn't let them down now.

In an hour the water truck rolled into the yard, and 500 gallons of water gushed into the storage tank. But all too soon the last of the water was gone. Uncle John and Aunt Etta realized that the truck would have to make many trips a day to provide the water they needed for the children and farm animals. So the truck rattled and sloshed back and forth all day between the water supply in town and the ranch.

Uncle John and Aunt Etta prayed while they

worked. The children soon realized that the problem was very important to their future, and they prayed for water as often as the grown-ups.

The next morning the driller came to check the well. He looked at the somber faces and big eyes surrounding him and searched for an easy way to tell them the old well was finished.

Uncle John said it for him: "No more water in the well, is there?"

The man looked sadly at the children and then replied, "No, I'm sorry—just dry sand. Look, I'll drill a new well, can't promise." His words almost ran together. "Pay me when you can. I'll start right away."

"How much?" Uncle John asked cautiously. He knew they had no extra money.

The man pressed his lips together and dug his boot toe into the soft sand at his feet. "Ten dollars a foot," he finally said. "That's cheaper than my usual."

Uncle John and Aunt Etta exchanged looks and nods. "We'll pay you. It may take a long time—I guess you know that—but we'll pay."

The man smiled and rubbed his hands on his dirty jeans. "I'll get to work then."

But several hours later he was shaking his head as he examined a broken drilling bit. He had already broken three. He had hit a layer of rock so hard that the diamond edged bits couldn't break through. There was no hope of a new well now, and he trudged toward the house to break the bad news to Uncle John and Aunt Etta.

The first shift of children sat eating their supper, and all looked up expectantly as he walked in.

When the driller told him the news, Uncle John shook his head again and again. "No, no, I just can't believe God wants us to give up. These children—most of them—have no other homes, nowhere else to go. We just can't give up." He spoke directly to the man. "Leave your equipment here, and try again in the morning."

The man held out his hands. "Look, nothing—nothing—can happen overnight to that layer of rock. No one in this area has a well because of it, but because of your other well I thought that maybe I would hit water before I got to the rock. I've done all I can."

"Let's take it to the Lord. He can give us water. Please just one more try tomorrow?" Uncle John pleaded.

The man threw up his hands. "All right, one more try tomorrow, but it won't do any good. I've drilled wells for years around here. It just can't be done."

Uncle John and Aunt Etta gathered their "family" for evening worship and told them about the situation. Soon a prayer circle was formed. Through the night they continued their prayers, Aunt Etta taking time occasionally to tuck away to bed a smaller one who had fallen asleep.

At 7:00 the next morning the driller drove up in his big truck. He found Uncle John, Aunt Etta, and the older children waiting by the well.

He looked at them with a mixture of hope and despair. "I sure wish it would work, kids," he said as he lowered his bit into the drilled hole and began adding lengths of pipe.

After a few minutes' drilling he added another length of pipe. "Must have forgotten how far down I went," he said in a puzzled voice. When he had used all the pipe, he started pulling it back up, saying, "I couldn't have made that much of a mistake!" The pipe and bit emerged covered with sandy mud. The man stared at it and exclaimed, "Mud? That was rock last night. It can't be mud!"

Aunt Etta began to cry softly, and Uncle John hugged her with one arm and several children with the other. "Try again," he said. "Is anything too hard for the Lord?"

In a few days the new well was gushing clear, cold, wonderful, abundant water.

The driller packed up his tools in the truck and stopped at the house to say goodbye to Uncle John and Aunt Etta. He found them on their knees, a slip of paper in Uncle John's hand.

Uncle John rose to his feet, tears running down his cheeks. "We asked for water. We never asked for the money to pay for it. But we just received a check from a man we've never met. It's just enough to pay for the drilling."

Uncle John signed the check over to the driller and waved to him from the porch of the house as he drove away.

Many years later, the well still pours out cold, clean water for 90 children who live with Uncle John and Aunt Etta. Through the years more than 600 children have lived in the big old farmhouse and the other houses that have been built around it. And all of them have heard the story of the wonderful well and have drunk of its wonderful water.

15

Shark

by Kathryn Wrote

What a muggy day," Kevin complained as he stared out the schoolroom window. He absentmindedly swatted at a mosquito whining by his face. Glancing back at his desk, he groaned at the pile of papers to be graded.

"What's the matter?" asked Bruce, a fellow student missionary who was sitting on the steps in the open doorway.

"It's too hot to be stuffed in this room. Let's go swimming or diving or anything to get outside."

"It's just as hot out there as it is in here."

"Yeah, but at least it'll seem cooler under the water! Do you want to go?"

"No, I'm too tired. I'm glad it's Friday and school let out early. I never thought teachers had to work this hard. I'm going to go back to the house and take a nap. But if you go diving, be sure to get somebody to go with you," cautioned Bruce as he stood up to leave.

As Kevin watched Bruce walk toward the mission house, he tried to think of someone else he might coax into going with him. But there wasn't anybody else on the island who knew how to snorkel.

"Well, I can go alone if I just float in some of the shallow water and don't go out past the breakers," he mused to himself. "The ocean bottom is pretty, even close to shore."

Fifteen minutes later Kevin was running along the white, sandy beach with his gear, looking for a good spot to dive in. Up ahead he noticed that the water looked unusually dark—that meant it was deeper. It appeared to be a long narrow ravine.

Hey, that looks good. It probably isn't more than 12 feet deep in the middle, and it's shallow at one end. There should be some good fish and shells in there.

Kevin sat down on the beach to put his fins on and to adjust his mask and snorkel. A voice of caution barely hummed into his ear. He knew it wasn't safe to dive alone, but he would be in fairly shallow water and nothing could really happen there.

His mind wandered back to a Sabbath afternoon a few months before when, on their way home from church, he and Bruce had come across two fishermen just returning from a morning of fishing. Hanging from their belts was their morning catch. Noticing two brightly colored fish on one man's belt, Kevin and Bruce had gone up to investigate.

"Good morning. May we look at your catch?" Bruce had asked.

"Sure. Nothing spectacular, but not bad for an old man. My name is Aungra."

"My name is Kevin, and this is Bruce. We're student missionaries over at the Seventh-day Adventist school. Is that really bright one a parrot fish?"

"Yes, I caught three this time," Aungra replied proudly.

"Don't you worry about sharks smelling the blood from your catch and attacking you?" Bruce asked.

"Well, we don't go out too deep. And with two of us, one is always on the lookout. There aren't many sharks around here, but you still have to be careful."

As Aungra finished speaking, his fishing partner came up to them from where he had been tying their small boat to the beach rock. He too wanted to show off his fine catch. He turned around slowly so that they could see the fish hanging from his belt.

As he turned, Kevin and Bruce noticed that one of his arms was gone from the elbow.

Aungra's partner followed their gaze. "Yes, I had a run-in with a shark," he told them. "It was three years ago, out past the lagoon on the other side of the island. He came up behind me, and my brother, who was fishing with me, didn't see him. The shark went by my side and grabbed my arm." He pointed to the stub hanging from his left shoulder.

"I had my hunting spear in my other hand, and together my brother and I tried to fight him off. He made another pass at us, grabbed my string that was loaded with fish, then disappeared out into the ocean. We got a good look at him. He was a big white-tipped shark with a deformed head. He's been seen several times since, but always on the other side of the island."

A chill had gone down Kevin's spine as he had listened to the story. He had never really been afraid of sharks, but he had a healthy respect for them. Twice while he and Bruce were diving, they had seen a group of small sharks way out in the deep water circling around in the murky ocean. They had been told by the natives that sharks never come in past breakwater, so that had been their rule—not to dive very far out from the breakwater. And besides, shark attacks were rare. In fact, almost nonexistent. Aungra's partner was the first real attack victim they had heard about.

This was too pretty a day to worry about sharks that weren't even around. The water bubbled around Kevin's legs as he waded into the dazzling blue ocean. The underwater ravine was a little to his left, and he could already tell that there would be a lot of fish in it.

A bright color flashed by his feet, and Kevin plunged into the water to follow the gaudy puffer fish.

Up ahead he noticed the dim outline of a grouper, a large fish but perfectly harmless. As he swam toward it, the grouper glided away and faded from sight behind a coral head.

Rolling over on his back, Kevin looked up through the water to the brilliant blue sky above. Not a cloud in sight. Some terns were circling overhead, catching the wind and riding it effortlessly. This was the life!

A few powerful kicks with the fins, then a glide through the water. Up ahead a school of fish—watch out, too late! He crashed right through the middle, making them explode in a million flashes of silver.

Below him on the sandy floor he saw something pink. Maybe it was a trumpet shell. He had been looking for one more so that he'd have three of them to take back home to the States. Fantastic! A perfect shell! It was one of the biggest he'd ever seen. The deep pink opening of the shell gave way to its creamy outside, blending together in perfect beauty.

Kevin glanced up toward the sky again and decided it was time to head back for the beach. Slowly he made a 180-degree turn and paddled toward the shore. But there was something off to the right, over where the water was darker. Kevin couldn't make out what it was. It was very still and from this distance impossible to tell what it was. The shell was getting heavy; should he swim for the beach or go investigate? Why not lay the trumpet shell down, go have a quick look, then come back for it? He dropped the shell, and it slowly sank to the bottom as Kevin swam off toward the object.

Suddenly the object moved, and as it emerged from the shadows Kevin knew he didn't want to investigate any more. His first glance took in one horrifying detail—a deformed head. A million thoughts flashed through Kevin's head—what to do when confronted by a shark, the fastest ways to swim, if his friends would miss him, what would happen to his trumpet shell . . . ?

If I can only make it to the breakwater, I'll be OK. If I can only make it to the breakwater, I'll be OK. If I can only make it to the—

Kevin was kicking as hard as he could, but it didn't seem that he was moving very fast. In fact, it seemed as though he was losing ground. Looking at the seaweed flowing in the water around him, he noticed something horrifying. There was an undertow.

Fear made Kevin's rubber fins move like they never had before. He felt as though he were trying to swim in a mass of jello. Progress was slow, so deathly slow.

The shark followed a short distance behind, effortlessly keeping up with Kevin's frantic pace.

Prayers ran circles through Kevin's mind. Kick, pray, kick, pray, kick, pray.

A quick glance overhead showed the first signs of

breakwater, but the shark didn't slacken his speed. He kept on coming.

Kevin was now in about five feet of water. What to do; keep swimming or stand up and try to run in the water.

The big white-tipped shark was closing the gap now, maybe realizing that the race was almost over.

Pushing his feet under him, Kevin began lunging through the water. Waves were breaking around him but right behind he could see the fin of the shark cutting through the white foam. He was too close; there was no way to beat him. His legs were moving in slow motion through the clinging water. His brain screamed, *Faster, faster!* But his legs wouldn't respond. "Oh, God, please help me. Please, I don't want to die . . . ."

Kevin heard an awful roar right behind him, and suddenly his feet were no longer touching the bottom; he could feel himself being lifted upward, carried over, almost floating. Then there was sand in his mouth, and he felt the wave breaking over him. Its roar fell to a whisper as it hissed by his body and the foam rushed by.

The wet sand felt wonderful under his palms. Kevin gulped in deep lungfuls of air as he crawled up to the beach. "Thank You, Lord. Thank You."

Kevin didn't look back into the ocean right away. But when he did, the shark was gone.

And somewhere on the bottom of the ocean lies a beautiful trumpet shell. A big white-tipped shark lazily circles around it, then disappears into the shadows of the deep.

16

Nightmare at Tuolumne Meadows

by Marion J. Prescott

This can't be real! thought Dan Johnson. Why had he been foolish enough to go out on his own? He'd been warned plenty of times by his counselor and by his dad. But he hadn't meant to be gone from camp longer than an hour at the most. Just a short trek up the trail, or so he had thought.

Now he was alone in a dark ravine with a possible broken leg, and night was coming on. A boy he didn't know had found him after his injury and had helped him. Even now Dan couldn't remember his name. Was it Joe? Yes, that was it.

"Thank You, God, for what you are going to do for my friend," Joe had prayed. "Thank You for the courage and the strength You are going to give him and me." And with that he had turned and left.

But you can't just leave me here! Dan had wanted

to scream after the retreating footsteps. But instead he called out, "How will you find this place again? It's—it's impossible! I'll die down here. I'll—"

"I'll find you." Joe's voice had come back from above him on the cliff. "I'll tie my scarf on this pine tree."

"You're crazy!" Dan had shouted. "There are thousands of pine trees up there—millions! How's anyone going to find that one tree!"

"Pray!" the boy had told him. "And start the fire at sundown to keep the animals away. I've left you plenty of wood and my canteen."

Now it seemed as though a great bowl had been dropped over the entire forest. All his life Dan had been secretly afraid of the dark. Now as his eyes looked up through the tops of the great trees, he caught sight of an icy slice of moon barely visible in the gathering twilight. For the first time he sighed a sigh of relief.

A moon! he thought. *At least there will be some light, and I have water.*

He lit the fire, and the sight of its glow instantly eased his panic. He ate some crackers, a candy bar, and an apple he had in his jacket pocket.

Lying back on his bed of pine needles, Dan did some thinking. Maybe things weren't quite as bleak as they had seemed at first, he told himself. Joe would be back with help by morning. He seemed to know the area well. And Dan would keep the fire going.

That would lead a rescue party to him. What a story it would make! It was bound to get into the papers. "Hiker Lost in the High Sierras" or "Lone Hiker Lost at Tuolumne Meadows" or perhaps—

Once again he glanced up at the moon, but this time he scowled. There were dark clouds around it. When he'd looked before, there had been no clouds at all. With a long stick he poked at the crumbling log on the fire and watched it as it fell apart.

Time was something he could only guess at. Hours had passed, he was sure, but how many he had no idea. Maybe he had dozed, but he didn't think so. His leg hurt. He added a piece of wood to the fire, and slowly his eyes grew heavy. But of course, sleep was out! He'd have to stay awake and tend the fire. But a rest—just a short *rest* for his tired eyes, he told himself, might do him a lot of . . .

What actually woke him was the sound of someone or something close, too close! The darkness mocked him. He could hear the crackling of dry leaves, the snapping of twigs, and an eerie rustling in the underbrush.

He felt his head. It was hot and feverish. The pain in his knee was intense. And the fire! It was almost out.

Thrusting himself up and dragging his injured leg along, Dan managed to reach the remaining pile of wood. But too fast, too hurriedly, he flung an armful onto the smoldering embers. He watched the sparks fly up, then die.

I've killed it! he thought. *The fire is out!*

Reaching for his pack of matches Dan set about trying to relight the fire, but he was too nervous. After eight or nine tries he crawled back into his sleeping bag. Once again he heard the faint prowling of some animal. A gasp muffled itself in his throat. He'd never been so completely alone in his life.

The moon was off-again-on-again. At times it was completely obliterated by the clouds. He looked up. A drop of rain fell on his trembling hand.

"Oh, no!" he groaned. "Not rain on top of everything else." Slowly he reached for the canteen, opened it, and put it to his parched lips.

Another rustle from the underbrush startled him, and he dropped his canteen, spilling its contents onto the ground. The rain pelted over him, adding to his misery.

Dan pulled his blanket over his head. No fire, no water, no food, no moon—and the rain was getting heavier by the minute.

Painfully he dragged himself to some brush and crawled under it. Only one person in the whole world knew where he was. If Joe had forgotten, if he had lost his way, or if the scarf had blown off the tree—

"Thank You, God, for what You are going to do for my friend!" The remembered words slid across Dan's mind as he thought about Joe's prayer. "Thank You for the courage and the strength—"

Courage and strength! he thought hopelessly. Courage! He'd had nothing but fear, and a conceited and ridiculous idea of perhaps getting his name into the newspapers. What about Joe out there? Dan hadn't even thought about his safety. What if he had fallen in the dark? He'd even given up his canteen.

Strength! Why had Joe prayed like that? he wondered feverishly. Why had he prayed as though strength and courage were already a reality, when actually—

Then suddenly he felt himself growing dizzy.

"Help me, God!" Dan whispered, amazed at his own words. For the first time since he was 9 years old he was praying.

He remembered the last time. He'd been with friends and had offered a prayer over lunch, and they had snickered. "That's corny!" one of them had said. "Do you mean you actually believe in that religion stuff?"

He had been humiliated. And he had never prayed since. Till now.

"Thank You, God, for what You are going to do," Dan prayed again. "Please get Joe here safely. And help me even though there's no fire, and no moon."

That's the last thing he remembered until he felt strong hands and arms lifting him into a wire stretcher. Until he felt someone putting water to his lips. It was Joe.

"I—I was scared," Dan said.

"I was too," said Joe.

"And then I—"

"I know." Joe smiled. "We heard you praying. You were delirious, but you were thanking God for His help."

"When I prayed the prayer you prayed, I knew somehow that I—that you—"

Joe smiled. "God promises us His help, so why not thank Him in advance?"

There were six men on the rescue team. They splinted the injured leg, then expertly hoisted the stretcher up the side of the cliff. As they reached the top, Dan saw Joe's red kerchief tied to the old pine.

"Ten million pine trees," he laughed, "and you were able to find *this* one!"

"With God's help that's the way it works. Here, take it as a souvenir," he said, untying it and sticking it in Dan's hand.

A helicopter was waiting in the first clearing. Soon it was moving. The nightmare and the darkness were a faraway dream. But to Dan, God would always be real.

17

The Lost Purse

by Florence M. Weslake

Derek, would you please go down to the grocery store and get me a few things?" his mom asked when he got back from school.

"Sure, Mom," Derek replied. "What do you want from the store?"

"Here's the list, and here's the purse with money in it. Do be careful with it. And please drop in at Auntie's on the way and give her this paper I promised her."

Derek put away his books and started off toward the store. After crossing the road, he walked under the railway bridge and came near the field where some of his friends were playing ball.

"Derek, come join us!" they shouted.

"I can't stop now," he called back. "I have to get some groceries for my mom. But I'll hurry, so I can play when I get back."

On he went, waving to some men who were repairing a weak spot in the road. Soon he arrived at his aunt's house and delivered the paper for his mom. Then he continued on to the store.

When he was ready to pay for the groceries, Derek felt in his pocket for the purse, but it was missing! He searched frantically, turning out all his pockets, but it was nowhere to be found. Maybe he had lost it at his aunt's house. He hurried back the way he had come.

Derek's aunt was also distressed when she learned about the loss. The two of them searched the house, the front yard, and the street—but to no avail.

"Did you stop anywhere else?" Auntie asked.

"No, I was in a hurry," Derek answered.

"Did you take anything out of your pocket?"

"No, I don't think so."

Auntie smiled reassuringly. "Don't worry. We'll pray that you'll find the money again, and I'm sure God will help us out."

Derek and his aunt knelt down and asked God to help them solve their problem. When they had finished praying, Auntie handed Derek some money. "Here, take this, and get the things your mom wants. She can pay me back later. I'm sure your lost money will be found."

In spite of Auntie's confidence, Derek wasn't happy. With a heavy heart he bought the groceries and headed home to tell Mom what had happened.

"Auntie thinks God will send the money back. I hope He does. Do you think He will, Mom?"

Derek's mom just sighed. She couldn't afford to lose any money. But since there was nothing she could do, she turned her attention to preparing the evening meal.

The sun was just beginning to set when Derek's mom stepped outside to call the children in for supper. Her face still wore a worried look as she called, "Come, children. Wash your hands, and we'll eat."

Then noticing that the gate was open, she asked Derek to close it. But before Derek could reach the gate, a black dog darted inside, wagging his tail and looking pleased with himself. He ran up to Derek and dropped something at his feet.

The boy quickly stooped down and picked it up. He stared at the object in his hands for a second, hardly believing what he saw. It was the lost purse! He opened it—almost reverently. There was the money inside, just as Mom had given it to him.

"Mom, Mom, here's the purse," Derek exclaimed, handing it to her. "This little dog brought it here! God *did* send the money back to us."

The family crowded around the dog. "He doesn't live on our street," Mom remarked. "How did he know that the purse belonged here?"

"Maybe the dog didn't know, but God did," Derek said. "Auntie was sure that He would help us."

"Let's thank Him right now," Mom suggested. And together they bowed their heads and thanked God for answering their prayers.

18

Surprise Bike

by Susan L. Skinner

Scotty really wants a bike for Christmas," Father said as he looked out the kitchen window at his two sons. Scotty and his older brother, Warren, were riding double on Warren's bike.

Mother had been watching the boys too. "I wish we could afford to buy one for him."

"Well, Scotty is going to get his bike for Christmas somehow," Father said. He went to the cupboard where Mother kept a jar hidden in the back. He counted out the money in the jar—musty coins. "There's only $13.45," he said with tears in his eyes, "but I know God will answer our prayers."

"It's not your fault," Mother said as she quietly put the money back into the jar. "If the layoff at the sawmill hadn't happened, we would have had a whole jar full. Scotty won't mind waiting another year for his bike. He's a very understanding boy."

Father put the jar back in the cupboard and silently walked out of the kitchen.

A few minutes later Scotty and Warren came into the house singing and talking about Christmas.

It seems as though they're never aware of how little money we have, thought Mother. *But they never complain or ask for expensive things.*

She stopped peeling potatoes and bowed her head. "Help us, dear Lord, to find a way to get Scotty a bike of his own. Not only would it make him happy, but it would also cheer up his father." Mother whispered "Amen" and left it in God's hands. He had answered her prayers so many times before.

"Can we go with you?" asked the boys when they saw Father loading up the old truck with trash.

"No, not this time. It's getting late, and you both have school tomorrow. Next time, OK?"

"All right," they said, a little disappointed.

When Father got to the dump, another truck, driven by an old man, pulled in beside him. He noticed that the old man seemed to be having trouble unloading. "Do you need some help?" he asked.

"I could use a hand with this," the old man replied.

When Father saw the problem he could hardly believe his eyes. There in the back of the truck was a bike in almost perfect shape. He quickly mentioned how much his son wanted a bike. The old man smiled as he drove off, leaving Father with a bicycle that needed only a wash job to make it look like new.

Father hurried home and shared the good news with Mother. "God sometimes answers prayers in unusual ways," he remarked.

"And in unusual places!" added Mother.

19

Prayer for a What?

by Veralee Wiggins

Mom, come quick! Bill just ran over Thor. Hurry!" Perri almost tripped over the coffee table as she bolted through the front door. Breathless and frightened, she could hardly get the words out.

Mom dropped her dishcloth on the counter and raced out the door behind Perri. There Thor lay on his side, flat on the ground. The treasured family pet—a beautiful seal point Siamese cat.

Fifteen-year-old Bill was on his hands and knees looking sorrowfully at his little friend. He had been backing the pickup into position to hook up the camping trailer for the church campout when the accident had happened.

"Mom, he's still breathing. What can we do?" Bill asked.

"Get a cardboard box. We'll have to take him to

the vet," Mom said as matter-of-factly as she could, trying to keep everyone calm.

Bill had the box almost before Mom finished asking for it. He took off his shirt and put it in the box for Thor to lie on. Mom, Bill, and 12-year-old Perri carefully slid their hands under the soft little body and ever so gently lifted the cat into the box.

"You drive, Mom," Bill said through clenched teeth. I'm never going to drive again." He climbed into the passenger seat with the precious box cradled carefully on his lap.

No one spoke for a while, then Perri wiped her eyes and nose on her sleeve as she leaned forward. "Mom, it wasn't Bill's fault," she whispered. "He was backing up slowly, and Thor dashed out from behind the rosebush into the path of the back wheel." She started sniffling again.

Mom reached her hand back and patted Perri. "I know, sweetie; it's just one of those things."

The 12 miles to the vet seemed to go on forever, but they finally arrived. Everyone jumped out of the car, with Bill carefully carrying his small load.

When the receptionist saw the cat, she took them right into the examining room. The doctor examined Thor thoroughly and took several X-rays before he turned to the anxious family. "Your cat is pretty thoroughly crushed," he said sympathetically. "He has internal injuries and many broken bones. His chances are minimal, but if you want me to try, I'll do what I can. Right now I can only treat him for shock."

"Please do what you can, Doctor. We love him dearly," Mom replied.

As they drove back home no one said a word, but at least the trip seemed a lot shorter. A few minutes after they got home, Dad's car crunched over the gravel driveway, his car door slammed, and then they heard Dad's jolly voice calling, "Hello! Where is everyone? Are we all ready to go?"

As Dad walked into the living room Perri threw herself into his arms and cried, "Daddy, Thor is hurt really, really bad. He's at the vet's, and he may die!" She buried her face in his shoulder and sobbed.

Dad looked at Mom with a question in his eyes. Mom told him the details.

"Should we still go on the outing?" Mom asked him. "It would keep the kids' minds busy over the weekend."

"No, we can't go anywhere. We have to stay right here where we can know how Thor is," Perri cried. Bill emphatically agreed.

"OK, kids, you win," Dad said. "We'll stay home."

The whole family pitched in and made potato soup for supper, but no one felt like eating.

"It's nearly sundown," Dad called soon after the dishes were finished. "Let's have worship."

As the family collected their Bibles and settled

down, Perri asked, "Mom, can we pray for Thor? Don't you think Jesus loves little cats, too?"

Mom looked at Dad, and Dad looked at Mom. They knew Thor was very near death.

"I'll tell you what," Dad answered thoughtfully. "Let's see if we can find anything in the Bible to help us decide if we should pray for our kitty."

So they started searching the Bible, using the concordance. They sat around the table, all working together.

After an hour and a half they sat back in their chairs as Dad summed up their findings. "Well, we haven't found a text that says, 'Pray for your pets.' But we did find one that said He sees a sparrow fall, and several that said if we pray with faith, He will give us what we ask, and some that said He likes to give us good gifts just as we like to give our children good things."

"Let's pray for Thor," Bill said eagerly.

Everyone knelt and prayed sincere, heartfelt prayers for their little cat.

After praying, Dad said, "Let's read a book together. It will make the time go by. Go upstairs and find a book that looks interesting."

After a short search Bill and Perri came back with *William and His Twenty-two*. Bill handed it to Mom as he said, "It's not a gun, Mom. He had 22 kids. Can you believe it?"

They started reading, taking turns, each reading a page at a time. After Perri finished her page, she closed the book and asked, "Can we pray for Thor again?"

They prayed again, each and every one. Then Dad yawned and said, "I think we should go to bed. There's nothing we can do for Thor, and we won't hear anything from the vet tonight."

The night passed, and everyone was up bright and early. After breakfast Bill said, "Call the vet, Mom. Maybe he knows something by now." He dialed the number and handed the phone to her.

"Hello, this is Kirsten Peters. We are wondering about Thor."

"Yes, Mrs. Peters. I'm sorry to say your cat isn't responding. I think you should prepare your children for the inevitable."

Mom said goodbye, then turned to the family and gently said, "I'm sorry, he's no better. But I think we should start getting ready for church."

"Please don't make me go. I don't want to be with anyone. Let's pray. Please," Perri pleaded.

Another earnest prayer session left everyone reaching for tissues.

"OK, let's read some more about William's 22 children," Dad said as he opened the book. They read for two hours, went for a walk in the woods, prayed, ate lunch, and prayed again. Then they went through the same process all over again.

That evening after sundown worship the children insisted Mom call the vet.

After she hung up, she smiled wanly and reported, "No change."

No one mentioned TV that Saturday night. They continued reading and praying until bedtime.

Early in the morning Mom called the vet again. When she hung up she had tears in her eyes as she said, "He isn't doing well. We shouldn't be hopeful."

Perri was on her knees as soon as Mom finished. She looked at her family and stated firmly, "The Bible tells us if we ask, believing, God will give us what we ask. It also says He wants to give us good gifts. It also says He made the animals for us. Well, I believe, so come on."

Everyone prayed again, and then Dad assigned some chores. Bill would vacuum the floors, and Perri would do the dishes.

After the jobs were done, Bill and Perri wanted to read again, so the family read, prayed, ate, and walked—exactly as they had done on Sabbath. They finished the book at 2:30, and Bill said, "The Bible says we have to have faith, Dad. I'm worried about our faith. Let's pray one more time, and this time let's pray, believing."

A few minutes before 3:00, the phone rang. Mom answered as the rest gathered around, listening fearfully.

"Hello," she said, almost in a whisper.

"Hello, Mrs. Peters, this is Dr. Grimes. Have I got news for you! I checked Thor at noon, and he seemed so much improved I could hardly believe it. I decided I'd better try to set some of his bones, so I took another series of X-rays, and I couldn't find a single broken bone. I can't explain it. I've never made an error like this before. All I can find wrong with him now are severe bruises over most of his body. You may as well come and pick him up."

Suddenly Mom was crying so hard she could hardly speak. "Oh, Dr. Grimes, you didn't make a mistake. I'll explain it when we come."

When Mom hung up the phone she sank into a chair and covered her eyes and sobbed.

"What, Mom? Tell us, Mom!" Perri begged.

Mom looked up through her tears. Laughing and crying at the same time, she said, "He's OK! We can go get him right now. He's all well. I really don't believe it."

"Honey, I think the kids really taught us a lesson about faith," Dad laughed as he hugged everybody.

"I think we all learned some things in the last couple of days. And what's more, we've never been so close as a family," Bill said. "I think we have one more prayer to pray, don't you?"

They all went down on their knees for a joyful, happy Thank You, we love You prayer.

When they got up, Bill had the last word. "A horrible accident helped us realize some terrific blessings. OK, guys, let's go get Thor." He patted his billfold holding his learner's permit. "May I drive, Dad?"

20

Trust and a New Trombone

by Stephen Iijima

I can't tell you how excited I was when I started learning how to play the old trombone that had once belonged to Dad. I was in fifth grade and practiced every night. The fact that the case was old and the tone of the horn wasn't very good didn't bother me—at first.

But as time passed, I began to feel embarrassed about the old trombone. And as my playing got better, I realized I needed a better instrument to reach the high notes. Mrs. Guthrie, our band teacher, agreed with me. I began to dream.

Then I found out that a better instrument would cost at least $400. How could I come up with that much money? My weekly allowance for taking care of Fleur and Ezmerelda, our milk goats, wouldn't begin to add up to that much money if I saved every cent for years!

Furthermore, every time I spoke to my parents about another trombone, my brother, Tim, said he needed a saxophone and a guitar. I knew my sister's piano lessons were already a strain on the family budget.

So I began to pray for a new trombone—and I continued to worry. What if God didn't think I needed a better horn? Did He want me to be satisfied with what I had?

A year and a half went by. I had only $40 saved up. The next fall I would have to have a better trombone. I'd be in junior high school and would need to reach the higher notes. But I didn't see how I could come up with $360 more.

When Mom came down to my basement bedroom to say good night, we talked about it. "I think the Lord wants you to trust Him about the money," she said.

That made sense, so we prayed together.

The next day I decided what to do with my $40. I sent $15 to India for flood relief and gave $15 toward our church building fund. With the last $10, I decided to buy some chickens. Maybe I could raise chickens and earn money for a trombone that way. At least I felt a lot better.

That day a woman called Mom about some chickens she had to sell. I bought five at $2 each. I hoped they'd sit on some eggs and hatch enough chicks for me to sell. But would you believe it? Those chickens refused to get the mothering urge.

Then another friend gave me a hen that "wanted to hatch chicks." But when the hen got to our house, she wouldn't sit on eggs either! My chicken-raising idea was turning into a big failure. And there was still no trombone in sight!

"Keep praying, Stephen," Mom encouraged. "Remember, 'My God shall supply all your need according to his riches in glory by Christ Jesus'" (Philippians 4:19).

I was beginning to wonder. It was already summer, and junior high loomed mighty close.

Then one scorching July day I opened the newspaper. There, right in the middle of a splash about the next day's sidewalk sale at a nearby mall, was this ad:

SNAPPY'S MUSIC SHOP
Going out of the rental business.
All used band instruments half price.
Buy one, get another for a penny.

My mouth went dry. "Mom, look!" I yelled.

Mom came running. When she saw the ad, she was just as excited. "If they're used instruments and half price too, we should be able to afford one," she said. "We'll get there as soon as the sale begins tomorrow."

The next morning we pulled in the parking lot at 10:00 a.m. sharp. Right away I spotted the trombones on a table outside the store—three of them!

"Try them out," the salesman urged.

When I picked up the Getzen, I knew it was the trombone for me. It was a beauty! It played easier than the others. And what a tone! And yes, trembling as I was, I could even reach the high notes.

I looked at Mother. She understood.

"We'll take it," she said.

"Choose another instrument for a penny," the man said, pointing to an assortment of clarinets, flutes, and trumpets.

There were no saxophones, so Mom chose a trumpet. "We can trade it in on a saxophone later," she told me. "Tim won't need it till next year anyway."

Carrying the trombone to the car, I knew for sure that God did care about things, such as trombones. He had supplied my horn. And He had even cared enough to make it a beauty!

And do you know what? I sold those chickens and a couple more that had finally hatched for $20. That was a 100 percent profit.

So now you know why my shiny Getzen trombone still reminds me that God hears our prayers. Sometimes we have to wait awhile, but when the timing and our motives are right, we can depend on Him to answer.

21

A Current Affair

by Tom C. Stiles

Dark, threatening clouds filled the sky as the three young men pulled away from their campsite. They were headed for Lake Michigan's Thunder Bay.

"Quite a day to dive, huh?" Troy said bleakly to his two friends.

Fits my mood perfectly, Greg thought to himself. His mind was filled with doubts about both life and God, and he'd chosen this weekend to sort of "get away from everything." But even here the clouds had tracked him down.

"At least there won't be many boats out today," Larry piped up. "That means we won't have to wait long to get the boat off the ramp."

Greg let out a long sigh, then sat up. "Well, I guess it won't matter much what the weather's like topside. Once we're on that wreck down below, I don't care how hard it rains—as long as the bilge pump keeps our boat afloat!" A grin crossed Greg's face, the first of the weekend.

"So which wreck do you guys want to start with?" Troy asked his companions.

Larry pulled out a map of Lake Michigan titled "Shipwreck Preserves." Pointing to a wreck site none of them had ever tried before, he asked, "How about this one?"

Greg leaned over. "Yeah, I've read the description on that one. Let's do it."

A short time later the three of them were headed across the cold waters of Lake Michigan. By now the sun had decided to put in an appearance, although the waves were still running a choppy two to three feet. Larry pointed at an orange 55-gallon drum floating on the surface of the water. "There's the marker," he shouted above the steady drone of the boat's motor.

Troy pulled the boat alongside the buoy while Greg grabbed a rope and tied it to the marker.

"I'm glad we have dry suits," Larry commented. "At 110 feet this water is going to be freezing!"

As Greg donned his gear, he found himself wanting to pray for God's protection, just as he used to. But he forced the idea from his mind. God just wasn't going to be a part of this dive, if there even was a God. Pulling his mask on, Greg slipped into the water first, then waited for the others to join him.

Following along a rope that had been attached to the buoy, the three divers descended into a world of gray. As they slowly pulled their way down the line, their underwater world became even darker. Then suddenly it began to take shape.

What an incredible sight! Greg thought. *This is better than a Jacques Cousteau film!*

The rope was leading them to the foredeck of a picture-perfect shipwreck site! The masts of the ship were still standing, and the anchor chains led off the bow into oblivion. The ship's wheel was in place, just ahead of the aft mast. This was fantastic!

It seemed as though their exploration had just begun when the divers' timers began going off, signaling that the safe time limit had been reached. Reluctantly the trio headed back toward the surface. Slowly, as before, they became enshrouded in an oppressive layer of grayness. After two decompression stops, the three young men broke the surface of the water.

"What a great site!" Larry beamed, climbing back on board the boat.

"Never seen one better," Troy echoed. "I just wish these tanks held twice the amount of air that they do!"

"Agreed. Well, let's get our fresh tanks ready and head to another spot. I'll untie the rope." Larry edged his way over to where the rope was attached to the buoy. But the choppy water rocked the boat back and forth, making the task nearly impossible.

"Let me give you a hand," Greg offered after unzipping his suit. He made his way toward Larry and reached out to untie the knot. Suddenly the bow of the boat dropped, and Greg's head—and glasses—hit the buoy.

"Are you OK?" Larry asked.

"Yeah," Greg shouted, "but grab my glasses!"

But it was too late. Greg's brand-new, expensive glasses were headed for the bottom of Lake Michigan.

I have to do something! Greg thought, his head spinning. He knew that diving back to their previous depth right away would be dangerous; there would be a risk of getting the bends. He turned to Troy. "Look, let's get our fresh tanks and go to another dive site, one that's not this deep. You and Larry can go down while I sit it out. When you come up, we'll head back to this site, and I'll have another look around."

"That's OK with me," Troy replied. "What about you, Larry?"

"Have I ever turned down a dive?" he said with a smile.

A short time later Greg lay in the cabin of the boat, his friends in the water beneath him. Slowly his thoughts turned toward God. *Are You there, God? Are You really there? God, if You're somewhere out there, help me to find my glasses in this great big lake. If you do, I'll never doubt you again.*

After they returned to the first site Greg once again donned his suit and gear. Because the buoy had moved by now, he'd have to use the boat's anchor line as a guide. The chances of finding a pair of glasses on the bottom of the world's largest inland lake were slim. But somehow he sensed that he would be searching for more than a pair of lost glasses.

"You know, this job would sure be easier if I were wearing my glasses," he said with a laugh. Then he lowered his mask and slipped into the water.

Larry leaned over the edge of the boat. "Remember, you have five minutes of bottom time. Be careful!"

Greg signaled that he understood, then sank beneath the surface.

Hand over hand Greg pulled himself down the line. Earlier the group had made some calculations to help Greg know where to look for the glasses. It was all dependent on the direction of the current and certain other variables. *Yes, finding my glasses would definitely be in the realm of the miraculous,* Greg thought.

Soon Greg's feet touched the lake bottom. This time the line had not led him to the wreck. Instead, he found himself standing on a flat desert of gray, hard-packed clay.

Greg began a slow walk around the lake bottom. All he could see was a vast horizon of the gray clay. He turned slowly, checking out his surroundings.

Just then something caught his eye. About 15 feet away an object reflected in the small amount of late-afternoon sun. Making his way toward the deep-sea glint, Greg tried to focus on the object. Slowly, as if in a trance, he reached down . . . and picked up his glasses!

Greg studied his watch to check his air time. Kneeling on the bottom of Lake Michigan, he sent a prayer shooting through the grayness to his—yes, *his*—heavenly Father.

22

Fast Food

by Sharon Boucher

Rudy slowly closed the cupboard door and turned with a what-do-we-do-now look on his face.

"Find anything?" his roommate asked.

"No."

"You didn't last night either when you went searching through the cupboards."

"I know," Rudy admitted. "I just hoped I had missed something—anything! I'm hungry."

"Me too! We haven't had anything to eat since breakfast yesterday."

"Don't remind me," Rudy moaned.

It was summer vacation, and the two young men were in Panama City selling Christian books door-to-door. Rudy, who had just turned 18, hoped to go to the newly established West Caribbean Training School when it opened for the coming school year.

He had recently learned about Jesus and His second coming, and he wanted others to learn about Jesus too. By selling books about Jesus and His love, Rudy could tell others about Him and earn a scholarship to pay his school expenses. His dream was to someday become a doctor.

Rudy and his friend had come to Panama City from their hometown of Colon and had rented a tiny apartment. It was in a wood-frame building constructed as many of the Panama houses were, with a number of one-room apartments all facing out on a common veranda that went completely around the house. From here the two young colporteurs went out six days a week to take orders for the books.

Rudy and his friend had been doing quite well as they went from door-to-door. The people who purchased the books paid a small deposit when the order was placed and agreed to pay the balance when the books were delivered. The two young men sent the orders to the Inter-American headquarters of Seventh-day Adventists, but for some reason the orders were delayed.

Back then colporteurs didn't have the more secure financial arrangements they do today. They had to rely on the payments they received for their sales. And since the books hadn't arrived yet, Rudy and his friend couldn't collect the rest of the money.

Soon they had spent what little money they had.

And now hunger was gnawing at their stomachs. Rudy and his friend dreaded the thought of tramping the streets without anything to eat.

"We've done all we can," they agreed between themselves. "Now let's tell God about it." And they discussed just how God might help.

"We could start knocking on doors, and maybe God will impress someone to place an order and make an unusually large down payment," one of them suggested.

"Or maybe we'll find some money and won't be able to find the owner," the other projected wishfully.

They thought of several ways that God might help them. I wonder if He smiled, knowing that He had already arranged for their immediate need.

As they talked the two young colporteurs looked across the empty table in front of the window. And out the open window, beyond the trees, they could see ships sailing on tropical blue waters, and in the shadows crocodiles lay dozing in the morning sunshine. But none of this interested them today. Together they knelt and reminded God of their need.

When they got up from their knees they stared at the table that had been bare moments before. It couldn't be! It wasn't possible! Where had it come from? There on the table was a large platter heaped high with colorful vegetables, potatoes, and fish— plenty of food for two very hungry young men. It was steaming hot and smelled delicious.

Eyes wide with unbelief, the roommates looked at each other, then back at the table. This was uncanny. This was unnatural. This was too much!

The two bolted for the door and flung it open. A neighbor woman who lived a door or two from them was walking on the veranda. She heard the door open and turned to greet them.

"Good morning," she called cheerily. "I cooked our noon meal extra early today, and for some reason I kept thinking of you and thought you might like a home-cooked meal. When I walked past your window, I saw you praying and didn't want to disturb you, so I just set the food on the table through the open window."

Rudy and his friend thanked her. Then they stumbled back into their apartment, thankful that God had provided for them.

"That's how I learned that God doesn't need suggestions," Dr. Rudolph Rodriguez said years later when he shared this experience with his Sabbath school class. "God always knows what to do. So now whenever I talk to Him about my needs, I simply trust Him to take care of them in His own way. And He always does."

23

Verloren in Deutschland

by Russell Lewis

By the time they finally landed in Germany, Brad was exhausted, and every bone in his body ached. He and his dad had been on a plane from San Francisco for 10 hours. And even though it was mid-morning in Germany, it was after midnight at home.

As soon as his dad got behind the wheel of the rental car, Brad was sound asleep. The next thing he knew, his dad was shaking his shoulder to awake him.

Still groggy from lack of sleep, Brad blinked in the bright sunlight. They were parked in front of a large building.

"I'll just let my office know we've arrived," his dad said. "There's a park across the street. Wait for me there. I won't be long."

Brad's eyes burned, and his legs felt rubbery. He wanted to lie down on one of the park benches, but he forced himself to keep walking to stay awake.

When he reached the edge of the park, Brad decided to explore a little farther. He walked slowly through the narrow, crooked streets, looking at the tall buildings crowded close together on each side. Turning a corner, he saw a wide, slow-moving river. He walked along the grassy riverbank and watched the small boats. He was so fascinated that he lost all track of time.

Suddenly Brad realized that his dad would be looking for him in the park. He looked around in all directions, but he wasn't sure which way to go.

I think this street's a shortcut back to the park, he thought to himself. *I should be back in a few minutes.*

The narrow street jogged to the left, then to the right, then came to a dead end in front of a parking garage. "Wrong, wrong, wrong!" Brad muttered.

Retracing his steps, Brad took a different street. He could imagine the worried look on his father's face. In panic, he began to run. Down one street, up another, then another. Each narrow street seemed to twist and turn and then go in the wrong direction.

Brad's heart was pounding, and his breath came in short gasps. Now he was completely lost. He didn't even know which way to go to get back to the river. Finally he stopped running and closed his eyes. "Please, God, show me the way back!" he prayed.

Opening his eyes, Brad turned a corner—and

stopped in surprise. He was facing a huge square, and in the middle of the square was the largest cathedral he'd ever seen. Its steeple seemed to reach all the way to heaven. He could almost sense God's presence slowly pulling him toward the huge entrance doors. At the entrance stood a boy about Brad's age.

"Can you help me?" Brad asked.

The boy looked at him with a blank expression.

Of course, Brad thought. *He doesn't speak English.*

The boy gave Brad a friendly smile. He pointed to his chest. "Karl," he said. Then he pointed at Brad with a questioning look.

Brad immediately understood that the boy's name was Karl and that he wanted to know Brad's name. Brad pointed at his own chest and said, "Brad." Then he acted out picking up a telephone and dialing a number.

"Ah, telefon!" exclaimed Karl, his eyes lighting up.

Brad was surprised but happy that "telephone" was said the same way in both languages. He followed as Karl led him across the square to a pay phone.

Brad wrote the name of his dad's company on a piece of paper and handed it to Karl. Karl looked in the phone book for the number and then put some German coins in the slots. Soon Brad had explained the situation to the English-speaking secretary at his dad's office.

When his dad arrived at the cathedral, he swept

Brad into his arms in a big, strong hug. "Here's proof that God answers our prayers," he said. "I prayed that God would keep you safe in His arms, and where did He lead you? Straight to a church!"

Brad introduced Karl to his dad. His dad spoke German so he thanked Karl for helping Brad. Then all three went into the cathedral to thank God for watching over them.

As they bowed their heads in prayer, Brad thought of Karl praying in German while he prayed in English. Brad smiled as he thought of people all over the world praying to God in different languages. And God understood and answered each one.

It's true, Brad thought. *God's love is a universal language.*

24

My Heart's Desire

by Elisabeth A. Freeman

had been taking English riding lessons for about a year, and I couldn't wait to go riding each week. Oh, how I loved horses! I drew horses, I thought horses, and I dreamed horses. And having my own horse would be the ultimate dream come true.

My parents told me that if I saved enough money I could get my own horse. So I worked hard doing chores, baby-sitting, and cleaning the church to earn money. I saved every penny, and I often counted my funds. But it never added up to the costly price of what a horse, even a cheap horse, would cost.

Lisa, my youth director, knew how badly I wanted a horse. In fact, she began praying for me every day. I appreciated her prayers. "Rachael, God's not going to give you just any old horse," she often told me. "He's going to give you your heart's desire."

I loved it when she said "my heart's desire." It sounded so beautiful. But when I stepped back into reality, I was down in the dumps. I knew that I didn't have nearly enough money saved. Things were looking pretty grim.

One day my parents surprised me by saying that they would buy me a horse if they could find a good deal. I was all for it. Excitedly I read ad after ad, and phoned this one and that. But the horses were either already taken or the owners wanted more money than we could afford.

My parents tried to cheer me up by planning a trip to a horse farm with some of my friends. Within a week we were on our way. It was a bright spring morning, not a cloud in the sky. The girls were all excited and giggly. But my mind was a million miles away.

I had read an article in the newspaper about the horse farm we were going to. They housed orphaned horses. My thoughts raced during the two-hour drive. *Could this finally be the day?* I wondered as we pulled into the long circular drive.

But my hopes were soon dashed when I found out that all the horses were sick, near death, or couldn't be ridden. With long faces and heavy hearts we piled back into the van. The ride back home was quiet until my dad spotted a sign along the road.

"Hey, Rach, do you want to check out the horse auction?"

Looking up, I read the sign and said, "Yeah, I guess."

As my dad pulled into the long, winding driveway, I spotted her: a 3-year-old pregnant Belgian mare, grazing in the pasture. My stomach did flip-flops as I neared the fence line. Tearing a few strands of grass, I held my hand up. She whinnied and gently nibbled the tall green stalks from my fingertips. I patted her nose, and glanced back at my dad with a big smile.

But again I was crushed when I learned that the horse was too expensive and at great risk for having physical complications. I left in tears, subjecting the other girls to a silent ride home.

It was the longest drive ever. I was so hurt I couldn't even pull my head out of my hands. With each stop, one more girl got out. I barely managed to say goodbye.

Then we dropped off Melissa, Lisa's daughter. Lisa ran out to the van all excited. I couldn't seem to stop the tears.

"What's wrong, Rachael?" Lisa asked.

Batting back the tears, I explained, "I wanted this beautiful Belgian mare, but we couldn't get her."

"Oh, Rach, I'm so sorry. But you know, God's not going to give you just any old horse. You might have to wait awhile, but I'll bet God has just the right horse picked out for you. I'll keep praying."

I gave her a half-smile and hopped back into the van. On the drive home, I felt so down. Lisa was always so positive, so sure God was going to give me something. Why couldn't I see it?

As the days went by I spent most of my time questioning God and trying to get my parents to change their mind. Nothing seemed to happen. I began to wonder if God even heard my prayers.

For financial reasons I had to change riding stables. On the day of my first lesson my new instructor, Mandy, led me to the corral. There, standing before me was Andy, a Tennessee Walker. He looked up as we neared the gate. Up until then, I had never seen such a beautiful horse. He was reddish in color with a white mask stretching from between his big brown eyes to the center of his nose. When I reached my hand toward him, he snorted and gently buried his nose into my palm.

I positioned the saddle on Andy's back and fed the bridle bit into his mouth. He rode better than any other horse I had been on. He seemed to know what I wanted even before I asked. Together we were like lightning and thunder. As we cantered into the meadow, it felt as though we were one. Our bodies were in perfect synch.

When the lesson was over, Andy stood perfectly still while I dismounted. My mom arrived as I was taking him to the stable. She and Mandy talked while I took care of the riding gear. When I came back out, I overheard part of the conversation.

"Yes, he's up for sale," Mandy was saying.

"Well, we'll think about it," my mom answered as she walked toward the van.

I ran to catch up with my mom and asked, "Who's up for sale?"

"The horse you just rode."

"You're kidding!"

"No," she said with a smile. "And I think we can afford him."

Excitedly we hurried home to ask my dad. I didn't want to get my hopes up, but it was too late. I sat in my room, anxiously waiting for their decision.

Hearing footsteps, I swung my door open. My parents were both smiling, and Mom said, "You can get Andy." With tears of joy streaming down my cheeks, I hugged them both.

Later, as I lay in bed, I stared out at the sky. "God, thank You," I prayed. "You really do answer prayer. You're not giving me just any horse; you're giving me Andy, my heart's desire."

Andy came home the next evening. I led him to the corral out back and stayed with him until Mom and Dad forced me to come back into the house. That night I lay in bed too excited to fall sleep.

The next thing I knew, my mom was shaking me. "Rachael, wake up!"

I pulled the covers over my head to block the light. "Aw, Mom, it's Sunday. Can't I sleep in?"

"Andy's missing."

I immediately threw the covers back and sat straight up. "Mom, you can't be serious. We just got him!"

But she shook her head and said, "He's gone, Rach."

I jumped up and fumbled through my drawers. Finding a pair of jeans, an old T-shirt, and cowboy boots, I pulled them on and ran downstairs.

The back door was open, and it was clear to see by the broken gate that my worst nightmare had come true—Andy had escaped. Frantically I looked in every direction, but there was no sign of him.

Fighting back the tears, I shouted, "Andy!" as I darted up the drive toward the road. Wiping my eyes on my sleeve, I glanced one way and then the other, but still no Andy.

It can't be true! He just can't be gone! I've prayed and waited so long, and I've saved my allowance for almost a whole year.

As I scouted along the deserted paved road, I pleaded desperately, "God, please bring Andy home."

I searched every neighbor's yard and called Andy again and again. I must have walked a mile, but still no Andy.

Then the road forked in three different directions. Unsure of where he could be, regretfully I turned and started for home. Kicking the stones along the narrow shoulder, I prayed, *O God, don't let him be hurt or hit by a car.*

As I neared our drive, my mom came rushing up to me. "They found Andy!" she exclaimed.

As we climbed into the van, she told me that she had phoned the police. They had just received a call about a horse in a farmer's front yard.

Although Andy was shaken, he wasn't harmed in any way. I was so thankful that God had answered my prayer—again.

We've been curled.

Twirled.

Children can be so cruel.

Doodled on.

And telescoped.

Now in Color!

Yet even when we feel persecuted, we know kids are learning about God, His goodness, and His grace. Our riveting stories, challenging puzzles, nature tales, and fun facts enthrall 10- to 14-year-olds with the gospel. Make sure your kids get their hands on *Guide* every week.

Guide. An invaluable resource for molding young minds. Even if it does get a little bent out of shape.

See your Sabbath School secretary to order for your junior class. For home delivery, call **1-800-765-6955.**